APM Project Fundamentals Qualification Study Guide

APM Project Fundamentals Qualification Study Guide

Association for Project Management

FUNDAMENTALS

Association for Project Management
Ibis House, Regent Park
Summerleys Road, Princes Risborough
Buckinghamshire
HP27 9LE

Paperback ISBN: 978-1-903494-54-7
eISBN: 978-1-903494-55-4

Cover design by Fountainhead Creative Consultants
Typeset by RefineCatch Limited, Bungay, Suffolk
in 10/14pt Foundry Sans

Contents

Figures

FUNDAMENTALS

Tables

Foreword

At the heart of successful project delivery is the concept of professionalism; what the Association for Project Management (APM) describes as the APM FIVE Dimensions of Professionalism – a breadth of knowledge, a depth of competence, a track record of achievement, a commitment to professional development and accountability through a code of professional conduct. Demonstrating these five values will ensure a professional approach and lead to the successful delivery of projects, programmes and portfolios.

APM Project Fundamentals Qualification introduces candidates to the fundamentals of project management terminology, and is ideal for those wishing to gain a broad understanding of the principles of the profession. No prior knowledge or experience is required for the qualification, which covers areas from the *APM Body of Knowledge* including planning and scheduling, communication, teamwork, resource management, project risk management and project reviews.

By completing the Fundamentals exam you will not only understand these elements, but also how they interact, putting you on the path to professionalism and a successful and rewarding career.

Association for Project Management

Preface

Welcome to this guide. It was written by us – project management professionals – to help you learn about project management and to pass the APM Project Fundamentals Qualification. We have tried to write it with the reader in mind, in a matter-of-fact way, but also in an accessible way through numerous figures, examples, teaser questions and representative multiple choice questions. We've also included a story to help put some of the theory into context so you can see how it might work in practice.

APM want to do all that they can to help you to pass the exam and so do we, but please remember that passing an exam is much more than just collecting a badge – it could be the foundation for a long and fruitful career. There are many different ways you can further develop your learning, and whatever path you choose, we wish you every success.

John Bolton and Paul Naybour
Parallel Project Management Ltd

Introduction

This guide has been written by experienced project management professionals for those preparing for APM's Project Fundamentals Qualification, previously known as the Introductory Certificate in Project Management (or ICPM). The APM Project Fundamentals Qualification is just one of a number of project management qualifications supported by APM to allow individuals to study against a well-considered syllabus and demonstrate their knowledge and capability.

To pass the exam you should aim to undertake approximately 15–20 hours of study prior to taking it. This study guide has four main sections, numerous questions, tests and opportunities for reflection. You could consider going straight on and sitting the exam after reading and digesting this guide or you may consider yourself better prepared after a period of reflection and interaction with a tutor to help ensure that your own personal approach is correct. You may need feedback on whether you are tackling the questions in the right way, and getting a sufficient number of them right to boost your confidence of passing the exam when the time comes.

So, spend time reviewing the four main sections in this book and then practising the sample exam paper at the back. You may want to use distance learning from an accredited APM training provider, attend a classroom-based, tutor-led course, or any variation of these. It's your choice, of course, but the more you can do to prepare, the better.

The guide has been prepared assuming you have no pre-existing knowledge of 'formal' project management. Clearly, if you do already have some knowledge, you will find some aspects of the qualification easier.

How this guide is organised

Introduction	Describes the structure of this guide and puts it into the context of the syllabus and the exam.
About the exam	Details the exam: its structure, format and how you should approach it.
Sections 1 to 4	The first section covers the basic principles of project management and the main concepts. Following this we have grouped the various learning outcomes together roughly in line with the stages of a project, and these appear as the remaining three content sections of this guide. Within each of these four main sections we have collated some of the assessment criteria to make it more logical from a learning point of view. At the end of each of these 'chunks' there is a story line that helps bring some of the theory to life and refers to the case study – BikeWeb, at the back of the book. You will not be tested on the case study but on the theory behind it. At various points we have also included questions at the end of each section to encourage you to consider the case study as a practical problem to aid learning, and there is also a set of practice multiple-choice questions.

Section review	This section contains the answers to the multiple choice and other questions posed throughout the book.
Case study	The case study is designed to give you something to work with when contemplating the various topics and their practical ramifications. It also includes notes on the case study. If you have your own project, you might well use this to help with your studies.
Exam know-how	Includes exam hints and tips, and general guidance from APM. Also contains sample exam questions from apm.org.uk.
Glossary	A glossary of terms derived from the *APM Body of Knowledge*, with only those terms needed for the exam.

Terminology

There are numerous publications on project management. A quick web search will reveal thousands of entries for project management and related topics. If you tried to read them all it would a) take an enormous amount of time and b) probably give you so many competing views that you would become confused. So, which are important and which are not? A key benefit of this guide is to help you sort the good from the less relevant. We have been able to draw on multiple sources and experience to do that for you.

This guide has been written in a matter-of-fact way, trying where possible to cut through the jargon, providing examples and real, hands-on, practical advice on how to better manage projects and pass the exam. We have also included a short narrative in each section to try and illustrate how these principles work in practice.

So . . . where to start?

This guide is intended to be used alongside the *APM Body of Knowledge 6th edition*, published in 2012. You don't necessarily need to be completely familiar with this book, especially as it includes a number of areas that are not included in the APM Project Fundamentals Qualification exam, but it is a useful resource.

In addition to the *APM Body of Knowledge*, APM also produces two key supporting documents for this exam, the *Guide for Candidates* and the *Syllabus, Learning Outcomes and Assessment Criteria*.

Some of the guidance notes from the *Guide for Candidates* are reproduced in this study guide, along with other hints and tips to help you deal with revision and the exam. The syllabus is a very useful document, as it takes you through all the topics you need to be familiar with and in particular gives details of the learning outcomes. These also appear in this guide at the start of the section that addresses them.

You should try to obtain a copy of both of these documents to make sure that you have the latest information. Both can be downloaded from apm.org.uk.

About the exam

What is in the syllabus?

The syllabus provides the backbone of the qualification. It describes each of the learning outcomes and the assessment criteria by which your understanding of those learning outcomes will be judged.

The 10 learning outcomes that you will be tested on appear in Sections 1 to 4 of this guide and are listed below. They are those that APM considers to be pertinent to the modern project management role at the fundamental level. You may of course already observe or practise some or all of these, but recognise them under different terminology. Throughout this guide we have tried to keep things as consistent and concise as possible.

1. Understand project management and the operating environment

2. Understand the project life cycle

3. Understand the management structure by which projects operate

4. Understand project management planning

5. Understand project scope management

6. Understand scheduling and resource management

7. Understand risk management and issue management

8. Understand project quality management

9. Understand communication in the project environment

10. Understand principles of leadership and teamwork

Within these learning outcomes you will find the criteria by which they are assessed and, rather dauntingly, there are 62 of these. No need to fear, though. By using this guide and tackling them all systematically, you will find them very manageable.

What is the format and procedure for the exam?

APM seeks only to test knowledge, not experience or competence. Assessment is through a 60 question, multiple-choice paper on a broad selection from the syllabus. Please note:

■ the exam is closed-book;

■ you need to answer all of those 60 questions;

■ you need to score at least 60 per cent across all the questions;

■ each question carries one mark;

■ you will therefore need to get at least 36 of the questions right to pass.

There are two ways in which you can sit the exam – either in a room with an invigilator or through a process called remote proctoring. Either way, the exam is a one-hour, closed-book, multiple-choice paper, invigilated under exam conditions by a nominee of APM or observed by the remote proctor.

Full details can be found at apm.org.uk.

1 Project management principles

Subjects covered in this section

1.1	Principles of project management
1.2	The project environment
1.3	Project life cycles
1.4	Project roles

1.1 Principles of project management

By completing this sub-section you will be able to:

- define a project;
- identify the differences between a project and business as usual;
- define project management;
- state the key purpose of project management;
- list the core components of project management;
- list the benefits to an organisation of effective project management;
- define programme and portfolio management and their relationship with project management.

Define a project

> **Definition – project**
>
> 'A project is a unique, transient endeavour, undertaken to achieve planned objectives.'
>
> *APM Body of Knowledge 6th edition*

FUNDAMENTALS

Characteristics of projects

Projects are normally described through the use of a triangle diagram.

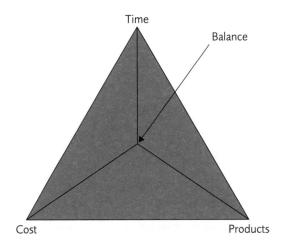

Figure 1.1 The project success criteria

In this diagram the three key success criteria for the project are:

Time – how long will the project take and when will it finish? This is normally defined using some form of chart or diagram such as a Gantt chart (more about that later). Taking longer than you should do for no good reason will generally result in a difficult conversation.

Cost – how much will it cost to deliver the project? This is usually described in a document called a project budget. Overspending against budget is not normally popular either.

Products – what will the project produce? This is about the 'stuff' that will be generated during the time and through spending the money (cost) that we have agreed. If you don't deliver what the user (or customer) has asked for, you will not have succeeded.

It is relatively common to hear the term 'quality' used instead of 'products'. This broader term (quality) is interpreted as 'fitness for purpose' and basically considers whether the products are what was asked for. In most projects the products are described in a document called the specification. The term 'quality' has the advantage that it implies that the products are not just any old products but the ones that actually fulfil the specification and will deliver the benefits expected. Together these factors describe what is called the project scope.

The diagram above is intended to demonstrate the balance between the various and sometimes competing components of a project. For example, there may be situations where a particular end date (a big sporting event opening ceremony, for example) is absolutely paramount. It must be achieved at almost any cost, although what usually happens is that the scope is scaled back to fit within the time and the budget constraints.

Some of the key components of a project are described in the list below.

- Projects are there to make a change. The organisation should be able to do something differently or new after the project that they could not do before. A new washing machine factory means we can produce more washing machines. This change is intended to be beneficial – the washing machine company will not do projects just because they can. The people who invest the money will want a return. It is rare to do a project without any expectation of benefit at the end.

- Projects are temporary in that they have a finite time in which they will deliver the products. This timeframe is sometimes in the gift of the sponsor or project manager but more often it is imposed from elsewhere. Our washing machine company may have an urgent need to launch a new product. Projects with a vital delivery date are a bit like a new wedding dress – useless on the first day of the honeymoon.

- Projects are unique. They have never been done before and may never be done again. Some may be very similar to previous projects but others will be totally new. The company may build many factories and there will be similarities but they will all be different (countries, designs, etc.).

- Projects can be of various sizes – from painting a house to building a motorway. The overheads associated with projects usually mean that project management is more easily justified as projects get larger. If a project is very risky, a greater degree of project management may be appropriate. The factory is a fairly large one; painting a house is a relatively small one.

- Projects operate within their predetermined and planned budget. Overspend will need to be justified – if an extra amount of money is spent, a return on that investment needs to be shown. The company will only have limited funds allocated to the new factory project.

BIKEWEB CASE STUDY

Throughout the text, you will find instalments from the story of the BikeWeb project. On page 165, there is a more formal case study about the same project. This explains more of the background and will help you answer the questions that follow each section.

Jayne was sitting at her desk on Monday, just after her project management training course. She had learnt a lot but, now she was feeling a bit daunted about how she could bring everything together to ensure the new website got off the ground on time. She knew Zak was quite eager to see it happen, and, as usual, whatever he wanted, he would have to get. In the past, though, projects had been done in a rather chaotic way, so this time she really did want to try to do things by the book.

She was disturbed from her train of thought by Karim, the IT manager, who came stumbling out of the server room clutching a crumpled energy drink can. "You look exhausted," she said.

"Yep, I've been here all weekend trying to get the database working again. This is the third time this year it's crashed. It was just never designed for these volumes. I've been on the phone for hours to the support people and finally got it back up." Then he added: "Until the next time."

"OK, well, when we get the new system sorted you can have your weekends back," she said.

"I'll look forward to that," he said, looking a bit sceptical. "What's the deadline?"

"It needs to be ready in six months' time, around Easter, for a race on April 23rd. We need it working for the exhibition stand at the start-finish line – they're doing a lot of marketing around it and getting people signed up there and then.

"We'll find out soon if we've got the loan, but Colin was saying the bank might want a properly worked up business case to show the benefits and that we can repay it."

"And if we don't get the loan, Zak will have to pump a lot of his own cash in – and you know how he hates spending money. If that happens, I just know he will be insufferably interfering."

"OK, I'll book holiday for May, then," he said. "I wanted to go away with my girlfriend – she's fed up with never seeing me." He looked at Jayne. "Is that OK then...May for two weeks in Greece?"

She squared her shoulders. "Yes, go ahead – I'm confident we can get it done."

"You don't sound convinced..." Karim muttered as he walked out.

"You'd better check with Colin – you know he likes to approve those things," Jayne called to his disappearing back as she pondered the end date of the project, a success criteria as her tutor had explained to her last week.

To be continued...

Learning exercise

Can you think of a project that you are aware of (perhaps from the media)? Can you write down the key success criteria for it?

Its schedule (When will it be finished?)

FUNDAMENTALS

Its budget (How much will it have cost at the end?)

Its specification (What will there be that wasn't there before?)

✏️ **Use this space to make some notes**

....

....

....

....

....

....

The differences between a project and business-as-usual

> **Definition – business-as-usual**
>
> 'An organisation's normal day-to-day operations.'
>
> *APM Body of Knowledge 6th edition*

Most organisations don't just do projects. They also have routine, day-to-day tasks to deal with. This is their business-as-usual or operations. Think of a high street bank. They need to operate their branches, pay their own staff, produce the customer statements etc. These are not projects, they are continual operational activities. However, if this bank wanted to introduce a new type of current account for its customers, it might need a project (or many) to create the new marketing literature, procedures, computer systems, training and so on that would mean it could launch that new account. These are projects. When it had finished, the bank would be able to do something that it could not do before.

Consider the following examples – which is a project and which is not?

- Open heart surgery.

- A factory manufacturing 300 washing machines a day.

- Building a new footbridge over a major river.

- Manufacturing vehicles.

- Implementing a prototype software system.

- Launching a new website.

Some of these are fairly obvious, given the earlier descriptions, but some are altogether trickier. Consider the heart surgery, for example. As the patient you probably wouldn't want to feel 'processed' in an operational sense; you are an individual and would want to feel more like a unique project. To the consultant, too, this (you would hope) would be the case. The theatre nurse, however, might have a different view, the anaesthetist another, the person sterilising the instruments another and so on. In these cases you would need to adapt your perspective to suit the circumstances. That organisations choose to create a temporary framework to control their projects is therefore a matter of choice, but they will do so to improve certainty of outcome and reduce risk.

Some key differences between projects and business-as-usual are described here.

Project	Business-as-usual
Seeks to introduce change.	Seeks to maintain a stable platform for efficient production.
Limited by time.	Repetitive and continues indefinitely.
Key experts employed to prepare bespoke plans and specifications and produce products.	Highly procedural working practices to enable effective continuity and oversight.
Specified scope of what the project constitutes.	The first few prototypes of a mass-produced item may be a project; thereafter they are business-as-usual.
Produce specific deliverables once.	Produce specific deliverables, but repeatedly.
They have a discrete number of steps (delineated by the finite time), called a project life cycle.	Products go through a life cycle from build, through operations to disposal, called a product life cycle.

BIKEWEB CASE STUDY

Jayne was thinking about the conversation with Karim from earlier in the day. He was working really hard, as the database was quite unstable, and he spent a lot of his time just keeping it going. The business had to keep running while the new website was put together and tested, but the current one would have to be kept alive as well, so the subscriptions kept coming in. The current business couldn't be affected during this project or there would be trouble. Jayne would need to build this into the plan.

To be continued...

Learning exercise

Think about the following examples – can you describe whether it is a project or business-as-usual?

	Business-as-usual	Project
A new aircraft prototype		✓
Undertaking market research for a new product launch	✗	✓
Selling tickets for a sporting event	✓	
Taking a family of four on holiday		✓

Use this space to make some notes

....

....

....

....

....

....

FUNDAMENTALS

Project management

Definition – project management

'Project management is the application of processes, methods, knowledge, skills and experience to achieve the project objectives.'

APM Body of Knowledge 6th edition

So, put quite simply, a project manager runs the project and a project is characterised by all of those things described earlier. It's worth exploring the definition a little further, though, as project management is not quite as simple as that. What does a project manager specifically need to do to run a project successfully?

When thinking about this, it might be helpful to consider the small website upgrade project in the BikeWeb case study. With this in mind, the core components of project management would include:

■ Ensuring that a suitable business case is prepared, in order to justify the investment. Before embarking on the project, the business case would specify how much the website would cost, what business it could be expected to generate and what might go wrong. By clearly stating these things, a rational view of the investment can be taken. It would also define why the project is necessary. And while the project manager might not be the one to carry this out, they are certainly responsible for making sure it is done. In the case study there are some indications of the benefits. See if you can spot them.

■ Ensuring that the various requirements are captured and properly documented. So, for example, the people in our case study will need to decide the number of pages, the content and the overall design for the website, probably driven by the market appeal and customer feedback.

■ Ensuring that a suitable specification of the quality of the deliverables – what the product must look and feel like at the end – is documented and agreed. Suppose the new website included the requirement for a mobile app. The company would need to decide what it would look like and what it would do, and these things would be set out in the app specification.

■ Developing suitable estimates and ensuring that they are within the bounds of the time and money available. In our case study, for instance, Jayne would need to know how long it will take to install the new server and get it up and running. If this is one of the early tasks, any delay will have a knock-on effect.

■ Ensuring that the project has the backing of the organisation and that suitable funding has been secured. The company is about to borrow money for the new website. Once the loan is secured, the money will be available and will need to be paid back.

- Developing and implementing a project management plan (PMP) for the project. This is the project manager's key tool. A good project manager will be seen clutching a schedule and they will be ardently keen to ensure that progress is made to achieve the milestones set out on it. For the website, Jayne will need to schedule when each of the parts are to be constructed – for example, the design will precede the coding.

- Leading and motivating the project delivery team. Quite early on in their career, a project manager will need to come to terms with the fact that they cannot do everything themselves – and nor should they. They will need to get others to do things for them. Collectively these others are the project team. For example, to make sure that the website is live on time Jayne must make sure the people working on it are focused and managed, and any issues are dealt with.

- Managing the risks, issues and changes on the project. Through the careful and appropriate application of risk management techniques and processes, the project manager will ensure that as far as possible all the things that could go wrong and interfere with the project are identified and dealt with. For example, the firm supplying the new server for the website in our case study may be in danger of going bankrupt (risk) and then maybe they do (issue).

- Monitoring progress against plan and making sure that any corrections to what is being done or how it is being done are carried out. If things are not going well (perhaps the designers in the case study are racing ahead of plan), the project manager must take steps to prepare the software engineers to build the website earlier to save time.

- Managing the project budget to ensure that costs are fully accounted for and that a proper audit trail is maintained. Importantly, though, the project manager needs to plan how the money is spent before committing it. Spending too much on one thing will lead to compromises in other areas. The work carried out by the team may perhaps need to be recorded on timesheets.

- Maintaining communications with stakeholders. These are the individuals or groups who may help (or hinder) the progress of the project. The project manager will need to pay careful attention to them to ensure that the project makes the most of their support and any negative influences are minimised. Although the bike company is fairly small, there are quite a few stakeholders. Can you identify some of them?

- Managing any input from suppliers or contractors to ensure they are performing according to the spirit and content of any agreements. The project manager will need to manage all the various suppliers and providers to ensure a smooth passage to completion.

- Controlling changes to the project and ensuring that any alterations to what is being done or how is reflected in any revised plans. This will mean the project manager needs to ensure the plan is continually kept up to date.

- Closing the project in a controlled fashion when appropriate, either early, where the investment makes no further sense, or at the planned end when successful. Once the website is finished Jayne will need to make sure the project is closed down, everyone is paid, all the last little bits are cleared up and everyone is happy.

FUNDAMENTALS

BIKEWEB CASE STUDY

That night, in the bar around the corner from the office, Jayne started to explain to a friend of hers, Bel, what she had learnt.

"Well," she said, "I have to run this project according to what I learned last week. We have to gather requirements, work out the benefits, decide all the things to be done, get someone to do them and try to keep on top of all the actions at once – and do my day job."

"Isn't that just what everyone does?" Bel asked her.

"Well, yes, I suppose it is. Juggle a load of stuff and try to get things done on time. The key to it seems to be this project management plan."

"Sounds grand."

"Yes. It's supposed to be a bit of a handbook for the project – nothing happens unless it's in the plan, and everything in the plan gets done."

"You'll need to be careful not to plan so much that you end up not getting anything done – sort of plan yourself into inactivity," Bel said. "People get very frustrated at too much planning."

"Yes, it'll need to be quite focused, or it could become just a lot of bureaucracy – and I've told you what Zak thinks about that."

To be continued...

Learning exercise

Put these project components into the order in which they happen

Element	When in the project does it need to be done?
Project management plan	2
End of project report	3
Business case	1

....

....

....

....

....

The key purpose of project management

The purpose of project management is to lead and direct the necessary resources to achieve the success criteria of the project including the delivery of the specified products to time and to budget.

As mentioned earlier, there is a hope and expectation that the successful delivery of the project (achievement of the success criteria) will have an effect, and this effect will result in a beneficial outcome for the organisation that is paying. Where there is an absence of benefit from the project, there will obviously be questions as to why the project was allowed to continue. Some projects are criticised long after their completion for not having provided any real benefit for the cost involved.

However, you should be aware that, although the project manager has a leading role in the delivery of benefits, these are really within the remit of the sponsor, who remains accountable for their realisation. The project manager may deliver a fantastic new office block, but if the marketing, sales and facilities management are lacking and people do not occupy the building, the benefits of building it will not accrue. Arguably this is not the project manager's 'fault' if they were not responsible for those aspects.

The project manager will also have no accountability for operations or business-as-usual. The project manager does not become involved in operations management activities, leaving this instead to the people within the organisation whose role is to be responsible for these things. The IT manager at the bike company will be responsible for the running of the IT systems.

FUNDAMENTALS

BIKEWEB CASE STUDY

Jayne was in the process of booking her first project meeting with Zak and Colin and was going over in her own mind what she wanted to say.

She was expecting them both to be reluctant to embrace all the concepts of project management, but then, they had sent her on the course to learn about it all (at least Colin – her boss – had). She was determined to try her best to make it work.

She opened the calendar system and looked for a date when Zak was in and she and Colin were free...

Diary date – project briefing, Friday 7th, 10:00. That ought to give her plenty of time to prepare, and they would be around until 12:00.

To be continued...

Learning exercise

What do you think Jayne was going to say to Zak? Write an agenda for her two-hour meeting with Zak and Colin.

Use this space to make some notes

List the core components and benefits of project management

For the project to be perceived as a success, and therefore for the project manager to succeed, the three success criteria shown in Figure 1.1 must be met. The point in the middle is the point of balance where they can all (in theory) be achieved. It is only possible to deliver a certain amount of 'stuff' (products) in a set amount of time with a set amount of money. If the customer wants more, it will (generally) cost more. The exact balance of the various components is what the project manager has to juggle throughout the project, after they have been agreed and documented in the business case and the project management plan. These two documents are discussed in more detail later on.

The project sponsor is responsible for making and agreeing this balance. They decide which products are produced, and how they satisfy the requirements of users. This is a fundamental aspect of a project sponsor's role and means they can create and own a viable business case (see later). The project manager may, of course, have a role to play here but they cannot on their own decide which of the users get what they have asked for. There may simply not be enough money to go round.

Some of the main components of a project management approach are:

- defining the reason why a project is necessary through the production of a business case and the requisite approval of that business case by the sponsoring organisation;

- capturing project requirements and documenting them in requirements documentation;

- specifying the quality of the deliverables through the use of product specifications;

- estimating resources and timescales using a number of techniques;

- developing and implementing a management plan for the project where all the project processes are captured;

- leading and motivating the project delivery team to deliver the work necessary;

- managing the risks, issues and changes on the project and making sure they are done through the processes described in the project management plan;

- monitoring progress against plan and seeking to correct any deviations where necessary;

- managing the project budget and ensuring there is enough to pay for everything that needs to be done;

- maintaining communications with stakeholders and the project organisation according to the project management plan;

- managing any outside suppliers to make sure they are doing what they have agreed;

- making sure the project is closed in a controlled fashion when appropriate.

Why do organisations want to go to the time and trouble of adopting a project management approach? Clearly there are significant problems with doing so; training staff, introducing governance procedures and processes to follow, structure, defined roles etc., are all required and inevitably cost money. To justify all this, in a nutshell, project management is mainly there to help with the management of risk. Things go wrong less and experience tells us that a project approach improves the chances of success, whereas the alternative – just doing stuff – is prone to lead to surprises, stress and failure. The table below describes some key activities involved in project management with a brief explanation of why they are beneficial.

Activity	Benefit
Understanding who needs to be involved	Means the organisation can recruit, train, redeploy or otherwise ensure it has the appropriate people for the job, thus avoiding delays through lack of appropriate staff. It can also manage cash flow, investment funding and other resources far more effectively.
Consulting with relevant stakeholders to understand the nature of the requirements and then achieving them	Everyone is clear about what will be delivered and when. Having signed up for the deliverables the users are obliged to accept them at some point during the project, thus ensuring they are fit for purpose.
Preparing proper plans to clearly communicate who is doing what, when	Everyone is clear on their role, there are no gaps in who does what and similarly there is no overlap or duplication.
Providing temporary but agreed reporting lines and accountabilities	Projects only exist for the time being, but the organisation has to ensure due diligence over how the budget is spent. Accountability through the temporary project structure provides this reassurance.
Management of risk and providing a greater likelihood of achieving project success	The sponsor and the sponsoring organisation have the assurance that there are no horrible (and potentially expensive) surprises that might compromise the project's, and even the organisation's, survival. Also, it is worth remembering that a risk may be positive as well as negative (i.e. things may go better than we planned).

 **BIKEWEB CASE STUDY**

"Well, Jayne, lots of plans and preparation going on – when exactly will we get started?" Zak was nothing if not direct. Jayne felt herself blush a bit. She knew Zak was one for getting on with things, but she had hoped he might be a bit more supportive.

Colin backed her up. "Come on, Zak, cut her some slack. We need to get this done properly. I sent her on this course so we could have a bit more certainty over the outcome of the project. We need to support her – it's really important we get it right this time."

"Are you saying we got it wrong last time?"

"Well, didn't we? The database was six months late, we missed the cycling season, we have got a system that is really flaky and it takes all of our time just to keep working. We need a bit more structure, a bit of planning and we can do much better this time around".

Zak looked thoughtful. "OK, let's run with it and yes, I will be with you, but can we please understand what the benefits of this project management stuff really are so that I can buy into it properly? Can you write it down and let me have a list of the reasons?"

A few days later, Jayne got a pleasant reply from Zak thanking her for explaining it and expressing his support for her. She felt good about that – perhaps there was something in this project management stuff after all, although he did sign off with the words: "Budget = £35k, time = 14 weeks, and it has to work, and there need to be a lot more subscribers and one-off customers!"

It felt a bit odd to have the responsibility for the project. Jayne had argued her corner and now she was going to have to do it but a week was already gone. She needed to get stuck in next week.

To be continued...

Learning exercise

What are the key reasons for BikeWeb running this project? See how many you can come up with.

Programme and portfolio management and their relationship with project management

Definition – programme management

'Programme management is the coordinated management of projects and change management activities to achieve beneficial change.'

APM Body of Knowledge 6th edition

FUNDAMENTALS

Definition – portfolio management

'Portfolio management is the selection, prioritisation and control of an organisation's projects and programmes in line with its strategic objectives and capacity to deliver. The goal is to balance change initiatives and business-as-usual while optimising return on investment.'

APM Body of Knowledge 6th edition

These definitions are really quite involved and technical. This section will try to demystify them. Consider this diagram:

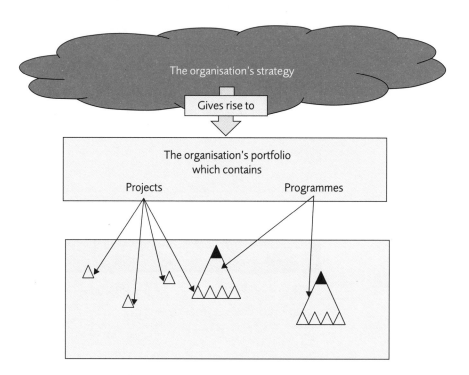

Figure 1.2 Projects, programmes and portfolios

Most organisations have a load of 'stuff' going on. They have to run their main moneymaking activity (making washing machines, printing newspapers, or, in BikeWeb's case, selling cycle routes). This is the organisation's business-as-usual (or day-to-day operations), as we saw earlier. In order to achieve something else (a new product range) it may have a project or perhaps, where one project would not be able to address all of these issues, it may require a programme of work. A programme is a collection of projects, but some projects exist on their own. However many combinations of projects and programmes it has are said to be in its portfolio. This is quite a simplistic interpretation but it covers most of the bases.

From the diagram you can see that the programmes have a number of projects within them. These projects are interdependent and will usually be multi-disciplinary (one may include some engineering, another, construction, another, business process redesign, etc.). Collectively they will be orchestrated to achieve a change in the business. A change in culture, perhaps, a different strategic emphasis (moving into a new market sector, for example) or some other more far-reaching ambitions than those that can be encompassed within a typical project. The exact projects contained within a programme will vary with time – some will start sooner and others later.

To help facilitate these changes, the programme would usually rely on the services of a programme manager, who needs to be a strong communicator, be able to manage resources and schedules, influence stakeholders and be comfortable with the uncertainty that a long-term, complex programme may generate. Programme managers have a number of key attributes (and responsibilities) that are different in proportion from their project management counterparts. They need to be strategic thinkers, able to operate within the higher echelons of an organisation, able to juggle multiple projects, with a highly developed approach to risk and comfortable with uncertainty.

Some examples of programmes might be:

■ A merger or acquisition in the financial services sector where one organisation merges its own people, processes and systems with those of another. Look for a key reason for this programme happening, e.g. "We want to be the leading supplier of XYZ services."

■ A car company developing a model through a number of key stages. This form of development programme is cyclical and the end result is never completely clear but, for example, to satisfy a desire to be a market leader will lead the programme through a number of product launches and upgrades.

■ Where there are a large number of diverse but complementary activities, with products that are not always clear or tangible. Perhaps one project might be lobbying governments to get funding for a charity aid project; another might be concerned with the spending of the funds generated.

Projects have significant differences from programmes:

Project	Programme
Constrained by specific objectives understood at the start.	Objectives evolve and can to a degree be modified as the programme matures.
Tactical single solution to single requirement.	Strategic in nature, tackling large change programmes or major changes in organisational objectives.
Projects deliver outputs which will subsequently deliver benefits after the end of the project.	Programmes will deliver benefits throughout their life cycle and have a highly developed benefits management focus.

Project	Programme
Focused teams with a systematic and structured approach with clearly defined roles and responsibilities.	Complex inter-project relationships call for highly developed communication and influencing skills.
A single customer defining requirements and accepting specified products.	Multiple customers at different times through their life.
Satisfaction of a single, tactical objective.	Top-down, 'visionary' approach, projects assembled into a programme where they contribute to the vision.
A known scope means a clear view of the necessary tasks is possible.	Cyclical development means projects can come and go from the programme as necessary (but always to achieve strategic benefit).

It is not acceptable for projects, or indeed programmes, to decide whether they should be run or not. This decision is in the hands of the senior leadership team of the business. There are some fairly basic questions that need to be asked (and answered) before this decision can be made. This is where the concept of portfolio management helps the leadership team understand what is going on. Some of the questions a portfolio manager would seek to address are:

■ Are these projects and programmes needed to deliver the strategic needs of the business (change)? If a project or programme is contributing to a strategic change, it should be in the portfolio. If not, then it should not.

■ Is the organisation confident that it can accommodate all the change planned by the projects and programmes without too much disruption in one go? If the tills are being swapped out at a supermarket chain, for example, it is probably wise not to introduce a new store design at the same time.

■ Does the organisation have enough resources to deal with all the change, or will we end up overloading key individuals or groups?

■ Is the risk profile suitable? If an organisation takes on too much risk at once, it may run into difficulties.

Portfolio management will also provide an overview and governance structure to keep everything on track and will instil an element of rigour.

Quick quiz (answers on page 148)

	Question	Options	Your answer
1	Portfolios can include...	a) Projects b) Programmes c) Business-as-usual d) All of the above	
2	Which of the following is not a project process?	a) Risk management b) Change control c) Concept d) Stakeholder management	
3	How many success criteria can a project have?	a) 1 b) 2 c) 5 d) Any number	
4	Which term most fully describes deliverables?	a) Products b) Stuff c) Quality d) Materials	
5	What does PMP stand for?	a) Project management plan b) People management plan c) Project monitoring plan d) Perfect management plan	

FUNDAMENTALS

BIKEWEB CASE STUDY

Jayne got a call from Adrian, the course tutor. "I'm just ringing to see how you're getting on after last week's course."

"Well, I thought your training was really good, and I am trying to put it into practice. I have got quite a few bits sorted and tomorrow I'm having a kick-off meeting. One thing you might be able to help with, though – can you tell me why I have a project and not a programme?"

"Wow, that's a bit of a question...Why do you ask?"

"I got a query from Colin, my manager, about it and I was a bit unsure. We got talking about things like the Olympics and why that wasn't just a big project. All I could remember was that programmes deliver benefits, but then I thought, well, actually my project will deliver benefits so there must be more to it."

"Well, Jayne, you are right – programmes do deliver benefits, but there is more to it than that. The Olympics was a programme, as it had multiple large projects, there were a number of large-scale changes going on, there was quite a lot of uncertainty and overall it was a lot longer than what you are doing, if I remember correctly. It is quite a complicated concept, though, so don't worry about it too much. How are things going?"

"Yep, so far so good." She was reminded of the story of the man heard to cry out just that as he fell past the 14th floor window.

To be continued...

Learning exercise

Is the BikeWeb work a project or a programme? Why do you say that?

1.2 | The project environment

By completing this sub-section you will be able to:

- define the term project environment;
- define the components of the PESTLE acronym.

Define the term project environment

> **Definition – project environment**
>
> 'The circumstances and conditions within which the project, programme or portfolio must operate.'
>
> *APM Body of Knowledge 6th edition*

The project environment

Projects do not operate in a vacuum but usually within a construct of national, societal, economic and other constraints. Take for example a commercial bank. It will usually be quite entrepreneurial, marketing-led and seeking profit. It will have a high degree of governance and regulation to adhere to and will need to be very responsive to the needs of its customers. A charity providing aid to developing countries, on the other hand, is not seeking profit; it is very cost-conscious and will be much more aligned to the greatest possible societal benefit of its activities. As well as external influences and pressures, a project manager may also need to bear in mind the internal environment of the organisation and its culture. For example, is it risk-averse or risk-seeking?

If you took the project manager out of BikeWeb and put her into a different business (construction, for example) she would have a different set of challenges. She would be doing the same things, but under different constraints. Understanding the environment of a project helps with the understanding of those differences and how they could be dealt with.

The project manager operating in these differing environments will face different challenges and potential issues. They will need to understand them and be able to respond to their subtleties so that the best job can be achieved. This concept of the project environment can be better understood through the use of the acronym, PESTLE.

The components of the PESTLE acronym

The context within which a project is being operated is fundamental to, and has a marked influence over, the way it is operated. The acronym PESTLE can be used to help analyse six components of a project context. Consider two example projects when referring to the table below:

	Construction project	**Implementing the BikeWeb website**
Political	A large, publicly-funded capital programme will have a large number of politically motivated stakeholders, and decisions on the strategic direction will be difficult to determine.	
Economic	Funding a large capital project is usually almost wholly dependent upon public funds (either directly or indirectly). Quite often things like Public Finance Initiatives or Private Partnerships will be relevant. Long-term projects are much more susceptible to the uncertainty around interest rates.	
Sociological	Projects need to be aware of, and may be constrained by, their position and impact on society in general. Power stations, bridges, railway lines etc. require a deep understanding of the sociological trends surrounding the project; this will make the stakeholder identification process critical.	
Technological	If the project is in a safety-critical area (e.g. replacing rail track outside a mainline station), it will require a much greater understanding of the technological specifications relating to the expected implementation timescales, specifications and anticipated through-life reliability.	
Legal	Significant attention to health and safety and other critical safety issues will be needed. For example, sectors such as the education and energy industries, have a very high degree of regulatory requirements.	
Environmental	The disposal of waste from a construction site is heavily regulated, partly to protect the surrounding environment. For example, a site such as a large brownfield development would need a very high degree of cleansing and preparation prior to actual construction. Clearly necessary, but it will probably delay construction and affect the schedules.	

So we can see that two different types of project have different contextual issues to deal with. Use of the **P-E-S-T-L-E** acronym is a means of helping to identify what they are. See if you can think of some areas from your own project back at work where these are evident.

There are other aspects of a project's wider environment you may need to consider:

Area	Impact
Procurement processes	May need to plan a long time ahead if procurement is heavily directed by the organisation or elsewhere (e.g. European Union Procurement Regulations). Procurement is dealt with later.
Regulatory requirements	Banks and insurance companies have to be aware of the regulation framework they operate in. This can place significant constraints over their projects.
Use of structured methods	In the UK, methods such as PRINCE2® or the Office for Government Commerce stage gate review process will be instrumental in how quickly or slowly progress can be made.
Appetite for risk	If the organisation does not have a large appetite for risk, this will have a big effect on the type and number of projects undertaken.
Strengths, weaknesses, opportunities and threats (SWOT)	The organisation needs to be aware of what it is good at and not so good at. Analysing these factors will provide a significant insight into how a project ought to be managed. Organisations with a poor record of managing sub-contractors may wish to run the project in-house.

 ## Quick quiz (answers on pages 149)

	Question	Options	Your answer
1	Which of these is not a PESTLE factor?	a) Political b) Risk c) Economic d) Sociological	
2	An example of a political context might be...	a) The price of copper b) The energy consumed c) The election of a new mayor d) The availability of leading-edge equipment	

	Question	Options	Your answer
3	A SWOT analysis considers...	a) Strengths, weaknesses, opportunities and time b) Strategy, wellbeing, organisation and threats c) Strategy, weaknesses, opportunities and threats d) Strengths, weaknesses, opportunities and threats	
4	Which of these is not a contextual consideration?	a) Project method b) Political c) Risk appetite d) Resource histogram	
5	The project manager should consider the project context...	a) At the end b) At the beginning c) All the way through d) Just after concept stage	

BIKEWEB CASE STUDY

Karim had left his skateboard sticking out from under his desk. As Jayne tripped over it, she was reminded of the health and safety module in her course. Karim and Lottie looked up. Lottie was one of the two analysts who were putting all the mapping data into the system ready for the new website. Karim had organised a separate server for all that, with offsite backups for added security. The data was coming from an agency and included the data they needed for the new route mapping. Jayne would have to make sure that the mapping module was integrated into the new website.

"Lots to do – need to get on," said Jayne. "Move your board."

"Whoa – hold on a minute. We were just looking at this." Karim held out a piece of paper with 'PESTLE' written on it. "Lottie found it in the coffee room and wondered if it was important."

"Ah, yes – it is best practice on a project to do what's called a 'PESTLE analysis'. It helps you understand what the project environment is: P is 'political', E is 'economic', S is 'sociological', T is 'technology', L is 'legal', and E is 'environment'. I was mulling it over at lunchtime."

Lottie chipped in: "This office furniture is so old-fashioned; we need more modern chairs. Is that the sort of thing?"

"Not quite," said Jayne. "You use the letters to trigger some thoughts about the project and how the different factors might affect what you're doing."

"Example, please."

"Well, here at BikeWeb the project is new technology, which would be an example of something in the 'T' category. It means we need to be super-careful about testing. See...the category drives some thinking – the result means we may need to do something differently."

"OK, so 'political' might be – what? I know – we need to keep Zak happy."

"Yes – that's the sort of thing. Internal politics certainly counts."

"And 'economic' would be the money we've got to spend."

"Well, sort of, except that's one of the success criteria. 'Economic' might be that we are expecting a lot of small transactions rather than a few big ones. We need to optimise the web system to make sure it's quick and easy to use."

"OK, so this is a bit like a crossword," said Karim. "'Legal' – tells us that we need to be careful of data protection for customer data and 'environment' reminds us that with a 24-hour server we need to be careful about power consumption," he said. "I tell you what – I'll come up with as many as I can think of and drop them by tomorrow – no charge."

"I'll look forward to it," Jayne said as she left.

To be continued...

Learning exercise

What do you think was on Karim's list? See if you can come up with six environmental factors for the BikeWeb project.

FUNDAMENTALS

✏️ Use this space to make some notes

....

....

....

....

....

....

1.3   Project life cycles

By completing this sub-section you will be able to:

- define the term project life cycle;
- state the phases of a typical project life cycle;
- identify reasons for structuring projects into phases.

Project life cycles and typical phases

> **Definition – life cycle**
>
> 'A life cycle defines the inter-related phases of a project, programme or portfolio and provides a structure for governing the progression of the work.'
>
> *APM Body of Knowledge 6th edition*

Life cycles come in a number of different styles. The most common is the linear (or waterfall) approach, which is explored in detail below. Another common life cycle is the spiral, where the products are evolved over a long period on a cyclical basis – like a new car launch, where the same basic steps are repeated for each new variant, or in other cases a life cycle called a V model may be a better approach. However, the linear model shown below is the one we will concentrate on, as it underpins the exam.

This model (Figure 1.2) assumes the left to right axis is time and that this high-level time factor is broken up into a number of project phases. These phases are described here, but please remember that this is a conceptual model. Your organisation may have a completely different number or set of names for your life cycle phases, but most project-based organisations will have a life cycle in one form or another. It is sometimes called a waterfall life cycle because it could be viewed as the steps of a waterfall, where water flows down the steps from left to right.

The concept phase encompasses everything up to and including the production of the business case. It includes the feasibility study and comparing various options so as to arrive at the chosen single solution for development into the project. It is overseen by the sponsor, and a project manager may well be appointed to develop the business case.

The definition phase includes the production of the project management plan and all the subsidiary plans such as the risk management plan and quality plan. It culminates in approval to proceed to implementation. The primary output is the project management plan (PMP). This documents the entirety of the project how it will be run and what it will produce.

Development covers the construction of the various components that comprise the end product of the project according to the plans constructed in the definition phase. During the development phase there may be many stages to allow for discrete parts of the project, a design/build engagement with a design stage review in between perhaps. The primary outputs are the products of the project.

Handover is the process of commissioning the products and the migration of them to practical use, and closure is the administrative closure of the project and disbanding the team. Products are the key outputs as this will be the tangible end product. Acceptance of them will be crucial in the overall acceptance of the project as a whole.

Some important points to note regarding the life cycle as depicted above are:

- Stage reviews take place throughout the concept, definition and development phases. These reviews evaluate the progress of the project against the agreed plans with the aim of identifying variance and corrective actions.

- At the end of each phase a gate review will take place. The purpose of this is to review the project against the business case and decide if the project should proceed to the next phase.

- An end of project review is carried out at the end of the handover and closure phase to ensure complete handover of the products has been effective and that project lessons are learned and recorded to inform future projects. Benefits (i.e. the productive use of the products) happen after handover.

Reviews are considered in more detail later.

Many organisations, and indeed whole industries, have a well understood project life cycle and there are also a number produced and recommended by other professional bodies, such as the Royal Institution of Chartered Surveyors in the UK.

FUNDAMENTALS

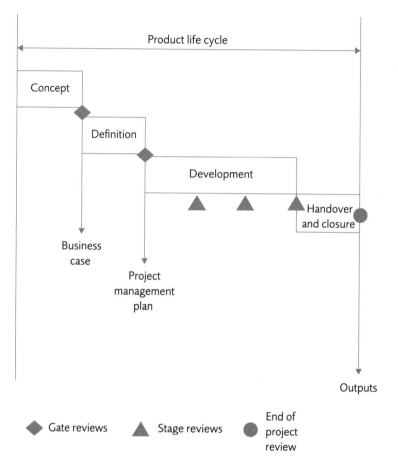

Figure 1.3 A typical life cycle

Learning exercise

These names (concept, definition, etc.) are not the same in different industries. Can you think of examples (from your own project experience or perhaps from observation) where you can spot one or more of the phases and what alternative names have been used? Note some examples here:

Use this space to make some notes

The reasons for structuring a project into phases?

The benefits of structuring a project into phases are that it provides:

- an easily communicable way of demonstrating the logical progression though the timeframe of a project, with clearly defined activities and outputs for each phase;

- an obvious point to consider stopping (i.e. between phases, at the end of one and the start of the next), where the business case and risks are reviewed and detailed plans for the next phase are considered;

- an understanding of which resources may be required (both in number and nature) and when. This helps the organisation to plan its resource requirements;

- the high-level initial breakdown so that detailed planning can be carried out (within each phase);

- an indication of when key project reviews can take place, ensuring the relevant approvals are in place and coordinated to proceed;

- assurance that proper attention is given to the early stages by demanding that the project goes through a number of phase gates;

- the ability to monitor progress, as we can link progress directly to them and recognise the completion of a phase. This will instil increased confidence in our stakeholders.

FUNDAMENTALS

Quick quiz (answers on page 150)

	Question	Options	Your answer
1	How many different styles of life cycle are there?	a) 1 b) 2 c) 3 d) There is no particular restriction, many industries have their own	
2	A project manager would need to understand the nature of the project and the industry it is in to make sure the life cycle is appropriate.	a) True b) False	
3	Which review happens between handover and closure and operations?	a) Benefits realisation review b) Phase gate c) Post-project review d) Stage review	
4	Who should the project manager consult when settling on the most appropriate life cycle model?	a) The sponsor b) Stakeholders c) The project team d) All of the above	
5	In the project life cycle, benefits are only realised...?	a) Before the project b) During the project c) After termination d) During operations	

BIKEWEB CASE STUDY

"So Colin, the life cycle we will use is this. Jayne scribbled a few lines on a piece of paper and put it in front of him. It looked like this:

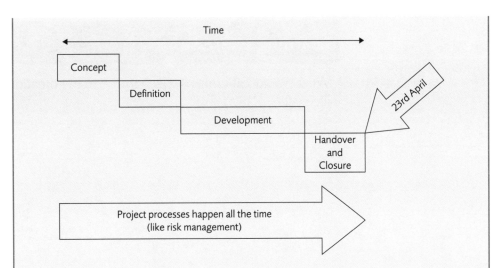

"At the start we have 'concept' – this is where we'll be producing the business case for the bank."

"Next comes what's called 'definition'. This is how we work out all the things we physically need to do to make sure the business case is achieved."

"Then we actually get on with the project. This is the bit where the work gets done. And, finally, there is a short period called 'closure'."

"So, what about testing, writing software, doing all this risk management stuff you've been banging on about?" asked Colin.

"Well, what you've described there are processes." She drew an arrow across the sheet from left to right. "These things happen all the time."

"Yes, but we don't do software testing all the time?"

"Well, no, but when we do it, we do it continually. It's not just once. These things – like risk management – have a process written down and it is that process that we follow. That is what the PMP is all about; I showed you that last week. It contains all the procedures to follow."

"So we write the processes in the plan and then we do them, rather than just doing them."

"Yes – I know it can seem like a waste of time, but can we try it and see how we get on?"

"Ok then, why not do a decent presentation slide with it on and we can put it on the wall. That way everyone knows where we are. We could put some rough dates on it, too."

"Yes – that's it; it's the first step in a plan, really. What do you think Zak will say?"

"Let's not worry about that right now – let's get a story to tell him first."

"You're starting to sound like a project sponsor."

"A what?"

To be continued...

Learning exercise

What would Zak's main objections be to the creation of a formal project life cycle?

Use this space to make some notes

....

....

....

....

....

....

1.4 Project roles

By completing this sub-section you will be able to define the roles and responsibilities of the:

- project manager;

- project sponsor;

- project steering group/board;

- project team members;

- project office;

- end users.

Project organisation

> ### Definition – organisation
>
> 'An organisation is the management structure applicable to the project, programme or portfolio and the organisational environment in which it operates.'
>
> *APM Body of Knowledge 6th edition*

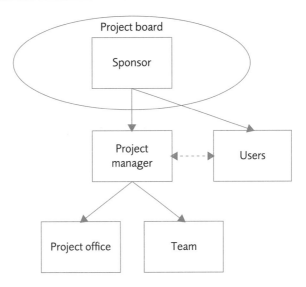

Figure 1.4 Roles and responsibilities

Who does what?

There is a fundamental issue at stake when we start to consider the organisational roles as shown in the diagram above. The project manager reports to the sponsor for the purposes of the project. This relationship is separate and distinct from any line management or organisational relationship that may exist. The sponsor could be the project manager's line manager but may not be and certainly does not have to be. The sponsor though, is the project manager's manager for the purposes of the project.

The team is managed by the project manager, who will manage each team member individually, and this will require a range of 'soft skills' such as leadership, motivation, communication, negotiation and the ability to handle conflict.

The users, representing the people who will operate the products and systems delivered, will need to recognise the authority of the sponsor. But they also have a dotted line to the project manager because, although the sponsor will have final say over the final products to be delivered and any subsequent changes that may be required, it is impractical to expect the project manager to deliver a fully functional and beneficial set of products without becoming involved with and having a viable professional relationship with the users.

In summary, the various roles have these characteristics and responsibilities:

Name and definition	Responsibilities
Project manager The project manager is responsible for day-to-day management of the project and must be competent in managing the six aspects of a project, i.e. scope, schedule, finance, risk, quality and resources. Well-developed interpersonal skills, such as leadership, communication and conflict management, are also vital.	■ manages the project; ■ owns the project management plan; ■ manages the team and suppliers; ■ manages stakeholders; ■ liaises with the end users; ■ manages suppliers.
Project sponsor The sponsor is accountable for ensuring that the work is governed effectively and delivers the objectives that meet identified needs. Owns the business case and the realisation of benefits.	■ helps the project manager manage key stakeholders; ■ helps deal with escalated issues and changes; ■ helps identify key strategic and business risks; ■ approves changes; ■ arbitrates between different stakeholder requirements.
Project steering group or project board The steering group provides overall strategic advice and guidance to the sponsor and the teams, communicating with the wider senior stakeholder base.	■ nominates the sponsor; ■ helps influence and manage key stakeholders; ■ supports and advises the sponsor; ■ authorises the business case.
End users (please note that the term 'user' and 'end user' are interchangeable) The group of people who are intended to receive benefits or operate outputs.	■ define what is required from the products; ■ accept the products (advise the sponsor); ■ operate the products; ■ liaise with the project manager with regard to changes; ■ accept the authority of the sponsor.
Project team members A group of professionals with a common objective, working collaboratively and in harmony to achieve the project objectives.	■ deliver the products to time, cost and quality parameters; ■ help identify changes, risks and issues; ■ support the project manager.

Name and definition	Responsibilities
Project office Administrative support in a number of key specialist tasks such as planning, configuration management and project data collection and analysis.	■ helps with admin and general support duties; ■ technical support including collecting, analysing and presenting progress information, managing interdependencies and handling communications with stakeholders; ■ assurance of governance structures and standard project management practices through audits, health checks and phase end reviews.

 ## Quick quiz (answers on page 151)

	Question	Options	Your answer
1	Which best describes the reporting relationship between the project sponsor and project manager?	a) The users b) The project manager reports to the sponsor for the purposes of the project c) The project team leader d) The steering group	
2	Who owns the business case?	a) Project manager b) Sponsor c) Users d) Internal audit	
3	Who owns the project management plan?	a) Project manager b) Sponsor c) Users d) Internal audit	
4	Which of these do the users NOT do?	a) Operate the deliverables b) Specify requirements c) Agree acceptance criteria d) Deliver work packages	
5	Changes to the project scope are approved by...	a) The sponsor b) The project manager c) The users d) The suppliers	

BIKEWEB CASE STUDY

Jayne and Zak were in Colin's office talking about the project. The business case was in draft already, but needed some figures putting in. The trouble was that Zak and Colin took different views of several points. They hadn't fallen out, but it was really difficult to get a single opinion from both of them.

"Zak, Colin, I am fine with all of this and I am confident, but we need to get some clarity about what is required," she said.

"It's just a website, isn't it? How hard is that?" demanded Zak.

"Well, I need to know what it will look like, the expected traffic of users, colour schemes, designs, functionality, loads of things. If I make it up as I go along, we will end up with a muddled look and feel."

"So, what do you propose?"

"Well, first of all we need to decide who is doing what. I have produced a little diagram portraying the different roles."

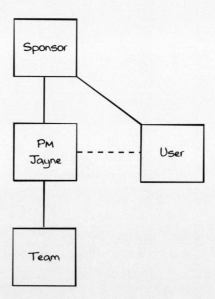

Zak and Colin leant forward and looked at each other out of the corner of their eyes.

"Look, humour me – you wanted a bit of formality, so here it is." She wrote her name in the middle box. "That's me, the project manager, but I need to know who I am working for."

"Jayne, you work for Colin."

"Yes, I know, but for the project it feels like you know what you want, and as the owner you own the business case for this, not Colin. That really makes you the project sponsor."

"Do I get my name on the wing mirrors, then?"

"Not that kind of sponsor. You own the business case, and ultimately decide what we are doing and take responsibility when it goes well."

Colin looked bemused. "What about me, then? I have to have a say."

"Colin, I want you to be the user in the project diagram." She put his name in the right-hand box.

"Why?"

"Because you run the business on a day-to-day basis. You need to be sure that, whatever the website ends up looking like, it will be your responsibility to operate it all and look after it."

"Ok, then," said Colin. "So we are in boxes. And Lottie, Yuri, Karim and Dean are the team."

"Yes, pretty much, but you need to give me authority over their time."

After much discussion, Colin and Zak agreed that Jayne would be able to use their time, but only once a clear schedule had been produced. Jayne went home that night quietly satisfied. She had written all of that up and put it on the wall. She would talk it through in the morning with her 'team'.

To be continued...

Learning exercise

Why do you think Zak was Jayne's nominated sponsor? Do you agree with her view of who it should be?

Use this space to make some notes

2

Project concept

Introduction to planning

Planning how the project is to proceed is a fundamental role of the project manager. They will prepare a detailed analysis of the requirements and translate that into a viable set of actions and products. Once the plan is complete they seek to ensure that the activities of the team are directed effectively at the delivery of these products. Meanwhile the project sponsor will be supporting them in delivery while also monitoring the continued viability of the business case. Some of this has already been covered, but some of the key principles are repeated here, as it helps to frame the remainder of the guide into the various life cycle phases (concept, definition, development, handover and closure).

Therefore, the stages of project planning during concept and definition are:

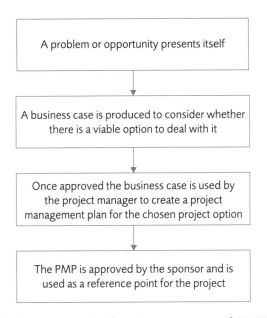

Figure 2.1 Links between the business case and PMP

FUNDAMENTALS

1. The users will generally identify a problem or opportunity that needs to be dealt with or capitalised upon, and this will lead to the creation of a business case.

2. The business case is used to develop thinking about many options and will ultimately propose a chosen option for consideration and approval by the sponsor and the project board/steering group. Depending on their perception of the relative benefits, costs and risks, the business case will be approved or not.

3. Once the business case is approved, a project manager will prepare the project management plan (or PMP). This articulates the way in which the project will be delivered, how much will be spent and when, who will do the work, when it will be done and precisely what the products are. It is a detailed document that becomes the cornerstone of the project from then on.

4. Once written, the PMP will need to be approved by the sponsor, and the project manager can then get on with delivering the project. The quality and accuracy of the plans will be challenged as progress is made and the PMP will represent the baseline document to be used as a reference point.

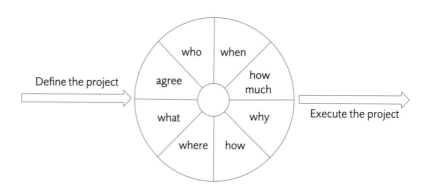

Figure 2.2 The project management plan

The PMP is finalised at the end of the definition phase. However, it may well exist in draft form during the concept phase, as the business case evolves, and useful information can be incorporated as the thinking develops. Much of what is in the business case feeds the PMP and provides background to the overall strategy. The business case will need to take account of the project environment and will be written with this in mind.

The project management plan is a bit like a handbook for the project. Anyone who needs to know about the project and the way it is managed or what it is planning to produce will be able to read this manual to find out all they need to know.

2.1 | The project business case

By completing this sub-section you will be able to:

■ identify the purpose and the typical content of a business case;

■ define the role of the sponsor and project manager in relation to the business case.

The purpose and contents of a typical business case

The development of the business case can be viewed as a process of funnelling. The problems or opportunities feed in at the top of the funnel, and they are considered and analysed to work out which of the potential options will be the right way of solving the problem.

Figure 2.3 depicts this 'funnel'. The ideas, problems and opportunities enter the system as a result of some initiative on the part of the sponsoring organisation. These may be problems the organisation faces (such as rising maintenance costs on existing equipment) or capitalising on an opportunity (such as a new product launch).

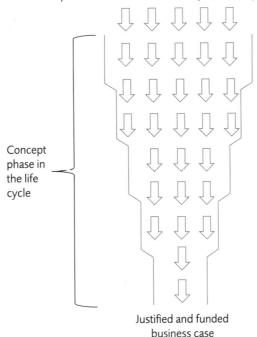

Figure 2.3 depicts text:

Options to deal with described problems/opportunities

As the business case develops, the overall justification and funding requirements for the project evolve. It becomes better understood and through the evaluation of alternatives and proper managerial and financial assessment the organisation can become satisfied that it has the best chosen solution to the stated (described) needs of the organisation. As the funnel of the business case development continues so potential solutions are dismissed, until only an optimal solution remains.

Concept phase in the life cycle

Justified and funded business case

Figure 2.3 Business case development

What would happen if we wanted to find a way of getting commuters across a river? A bridge could be built; ferryboats could be commissioned; a tunnel could be dug; helicopters could be used, etc. Clearly there are a number of potential solutions to this problem. As they are evaluated, so some will be discarded as being too costly, impractical, time-consuming or not worth pursuing for any number of other reasons. Once the evaluation has been done, the most viable single option will have emerged for the problem of how to get people across the river.

The business case balances the following three major topics:

Benefits – How much might be recovered from the investment, who will benefit and when will it be evidenced?

Costs – How much will it cost to produce the products that will collectively deliver the benefits?

Risks – What might go wrong with either of the above? A business case is mostly concerned with strategic risks (things that might cause problems for the business).

As well as these three things, the business case needs to include a number of other key headings:

■ **The strategic case for the project and why it is needed**. The BikeWeb project is going to solve the problem of the old website being too expensive to maintain and fulfil the need to provide more capacity.

■ **Options evaluation and justification of the chosen option**. As the funnel progresses, so the various options will be discarded in favour of ultimately just one. This one option is then taken across into the definition phase and a PMP produced. BikeWeb has considered other options and arrived at this one. The company could have outsourced its entire billing function to a third party, but wanted to keep it in-house to maintain control.

■ **The effect on business-as-usual**. The business case will, as far as possible, describe how the business operations will be affected by the chosen option.

■ **High-level description of the chosen project scope** (what's included and what isn't). The BikeWeb project scope includes the new site, new payment system, new map content and support arrangements.

■ **Expected benefits to be derived from the project** (which can be financial or non-financial) and any unavoidable dis-benefits (such as loss of a Greenfield site). For BikeWeb, the key benefit is a projected £100,000 increase in revenue.

■ **Commercial aspects** (including the costs for the project), an evaluation to see if the benefits outweigh the costs. Often organisations will have investment appraisal rules to check the financial return from a project against the costs. This section might also describe the funding arrangements for the project (such as a bank loan).

■ **Risks**. Initially, the strategic risks will be covered so that suitable mitigating actions can be taken well before the project proper gets underway. The main risk to the BikeWeb project is the failure to achieve satisfactory testing of the payment system.

■ **Target schedule** (key dates and milestones). This again will be a high-level schedule showing the delivery timescales for the products and the benefits. Possibly this will be just a list of key deadlines to be met and further broken down in the PMP later. The end date for BikeWeb is 10 months. It might turn out to be nine months and two weeks when the planning detail is worked out, but for now this high-level estimate will have to do.

Once written and approved, the business case can be changed, but only with the explicit agreement of the sponsor. It forms the baseline for the project and as such is a reference point for comparison during all future project gates and reviews. It may need to change as the project develops, but care will be needed, as all decisions based on it to that date may also need to be reconsidered and, if something happens that has a big effect, the business case may no longer be viable and the project may need to be prematurely terminated.

Roles in the preparation of the business case

The question is always asked – who writes the business case?

The answer is not absolutely prescribed. The sponsor owns the business case, but quite often they will not be able to write the document as they will probably not have the time, the knowledge or the data.

So who does contribute?

The sponsor oversees the construction of the business case in collaboration with the other roles. They may well have specialised knowledge but must remember to use the experts that work for them and not presume too much based on their own expertise (or lack of it). Sponsorship is a role that provides a link between the management level and the external environment. The sponsor owns the business case and is ultimately accountable for the realisation of the benefits. However, a project manager will usually be responsible for preparing the business case, possibly with specialist support from some or all of the following groups:

■ The providers and suppliers may well have significant detailed knowledge to make the writing of the business case possible; for example, they may be experts in a particular process that the client is unaware of, which will put them in a good position to add value.

■ The users know what they require by way of products and benefits; they need to separate 'musts' from 'wants', prioritise the relevant aspects of the specification and provide advice to the sponsor as to the exact details of some of them.

■ Subject matter experts, such as procurement specialists, management accountants, marketing professionals, drawn from within the organisation. These staff can be co-opted onto the team to enable proper analysis and decisions to be made.

■ The steering group will support the sponsor in the construction of the business case and will approve it.

■ Often external consultants will be engaged to prepare the business case for a project. This has the distinct advantage of making the decision-making process dispassionate.

At the end of the exercise, the business case should be something that all parties can agree and subscribe to.

FUNDAMENTALS

 Quick quiz (answers on pages 151–2)

	Question	Options	Your answer
1	When must the business case be checked for alignment to the project management plan?	a) During the early stages of the project, as the business case evolves so the PMP needs to be in preliminary drafts b) During the definition phase, after the business case is approved but while the PMP is still being written c) During development, when the business case and project management plan have been baselined and are subject to change control d) All of the above	
2	The business case is most concerned with which type of risk?	a) Risks to the completion of the project deliverables but not the realisation of the project benefits b) Risks to the completion of the project deliverables and the realisation of the project benefits c) Just the risks associated with the project delivery d) Just the risk associated with realisation of the benefits	
3	The business case, once written, may change....	a) Only at the end of concept b) By approval at any time through formal change control c) During the definition phase if it is incompatible with the PMP d) Never, because it has been baselined	
4	The business case leads directly into....	a) The production of the project management plan b) A scope change control process c) Development of the project schedule d) Definition of configuration records	

	Question	Options	Your answer
5	When the project is complete, who will sign off the business case as fulfilled?	a) Project manager b) Users c) Sponsor d) The team	

BIKEWEB CASE STUDY

"Are you ready?" Colin asked Jayne as he strolled towards her desk.

"Yep – all ready. I've done all the copies we need. I thought the days of going to see the bank manager were long gone."

"Apparently not. They are keen to see our business case before we get our hands on their cash."

The bank was just around the corner from the office and in 10 minutes they were seated in the little cubicle with the smoked glass door.

"Well, thanks for coming along. It will be good to see your plans for your new site – it sounds exciting." Mrs Fitzroy was the local business banker allocated to them, and what she said would probably be the final decision. They walked through the business case, and Jayne laid out a sheet on the table as something to provide a bit of an agenda. Her sheet looked like this.

AGENDA FOR BANK MEETING

1. OUTLINE OF PROJECT

2. BENEFITS

3. WHAT WE NEED FROM THE BANK

4. WHAT MIGHT GO WRONG

5. NEXT STEPS

After an hour of discussion and questions, there seemed to be a bit of a lull in the conversation and they all looked at each other.

"Well, you certainly seem to have done a good deal of preparation, and I think in summary you are suggesting that if the bank provides funding of £50,000, combined with your £10,000 grant, you predict an increase in income of £100,000 in

the first year, and this will grow by 10 per cent every year after that. Does that sort of summarise it?"

"Well, yes," said Jayne, and Colin nodded.

"OK, well, we will have to run it past our head office team, but I think we ought to be able to do that. I cannot guarantee it, but we will hopefully have an answer for you by the end of the week. Will email be OK?"

To be continued…

Use this space to make some notes

2.2 Success and benefits management

By completing this sub-section you will be able to:

- define success criteria in the context of managing projects;
- define benefits management;
- identify typical success factors that may contribute to successful projects;
- define the use of KPIs.

Benefits management and success

> ### Definition – benefits management
>
> 'Benefits management is the identification, definition, planning, tracking and realisation of business benefit.'
>
> *APM Body of Knowledge 6th edition*

> ### Definition – success criteria
>
> 'The qualitative or quantitative measures by which the success of project management is judged.'
>
> *APM Body of Knowledge 6th edition*

There are two complementary views of success here.

Take the sponsor's perspective. The sponsor is tasked with the realisation of benefits because they own the project business case, whereas the project manager is focused on delivering to time, cost and quality as specified in the project management plan. These do not compete, but it is important to understand the nature of the differences.

Take the example of a new road bridge over a river. The project manager can build the most cost-effective structure possible, on time and to budget (as per their project management plan) but if nobody uses the bridge, there will be no practical benefit, and any benefits used to justify the business case will obviously not be realised.

Question: is it possible to have a successful project which delivers to time, cost and quality that does not deliver benefit? Or, conversely, is it possible to have an unsuccessful project (one that overspends, perhaps) that does realise benefit?

The answer, of course, is yes to both. The difficulty, however, is that if we do not have a sufficiently well-developed understanding of each, we find ourselves unable to really classify the project as a success or failure.

Fortunately, the *APM Body of Knowledge* has a solution – but it does involve some new terminology. Consider the introduction of the BikeWeb website.

FUNDAMENTALS

Table 2.1 Success and benefit terminology

Term	Definition	Example – for BikeWeb
Success criteria	The qualitative or quantitative* measures by which the success of project management is judged.	■ Was the project finished on time? ■ Can we stream data fast enough? ■ Did we overspend?
Benefits	The quantifiable and measurable improvement resulting from completion of deliverables that is perceived as positive by a stakeholder. It will normally have a tangible value, expressed in monetary terms, that will justify the investment. Please note that benefits can be measured qualitatively as well as quantitatively.	■ People download the route challenges, which generates more income. ■ People sign up to subscription services. ■ BikeWeb grows and employs more people. They get paid a salary, which is clearly of benefit to them.
Key performance indicators (KPIs)	Measures of success that can be used throughout the project to ensure that it is progressing towards a successful conclusion. Please note that a successful conclusion will be primarily measured by achievement of the success criteria and delivery of the benefits.	■ During the project, Jayne might want to measure how the live testing is going, how many faults are reported and how fast they are fixed. ■ We might want to keep track of how much of the website has been completed against plan at a certain time.
Success factors	Management practices that, when implemented, will increase the likelihood of success of a project, programme or portfolio.	■ Is there a clear focus on the value of the work and are the team motivated to deliver it? ■ Is the senior management of BikeWeb fully supportive of the project? ■ Are the goals and objectives clear and unambiguous?

* 'Qualitative' refers to those measures that permit subjectivity, whereas 'quantitative' ones are more precise and require a purely analytical, data-based assessment.

Once you have defined the success criteria for your project, it ought to be possible to produce a set of deliverables and plans to enable you to satisfy yourselves that you can meet them. Thus the success criteria ought to be a natural outcome.

So there are a few things to remember about the terminology and definitions. If you grasp the principles of these here, the production of other project management material, such as the project management plan, will be easier.

 Quick quiz (answers on page 152)

	Question	Options	Your answer
1	The target finish time for a project would be an example of...	a) Success criteria b) Success factors c) Benefits delivered d) Change control process	
2	In a typical project we might track the monthly expenditure on the project. This would be an example of...	a) Success criteria b) Success factors c) Key performance indicators d) Benefits	
3	Throughout the project the project manager needs to keep a careful track of...	a) The monthly expenditure and the final forecast cost for the completion of the project b) The delivery of the project activities and deliverables in accordance with the project schedule c) The performance of the project in delivering products that meet the defined quality criteria d) All of the above	
4	Having a sponsor who is prepared and able to make quick decisions might be an example of a...	a) Success factor b) Success criteria c) Key performance indicator d) Benefit	

	Question	Options	Your answer
5	Reducing the expenditure on materials storage in a warehouse as a direct result of running a project is an example of what?	a) Benefit b) Success criteria c) Success factor d) KPI	

BIKEWEB CASE STUDY

Zak was eagerly awaiting their return. He had decided not to go to the bank as he wanted it to come across as a company approach rather than it being him asking.

"How'd it go?"

"Very well, actually," said Jane. "She listened to everything and will get back to us by the end of the week."

"You mean she didn't say yes?"

"Yes, but she didn't say no, either, she was actually very positive and has gone to talk to her boss."

"I hope you sold the benefits – how much we expect to get back."

"Yep."

"And how few risks there were in those assumptions."

"Yep."

"And that a key success factor is getting going as soon as possible."

"Yep," Jayne nodded again.

"And that we have to be finished by the race weekend."

"Yes, we told her that that was one of our main criteria for success."

Zak didn't know what else to ask, so he sat down, raised his eyebrows and just nodded. "Have to wait and see. then."

"Yep."

To be continued...

📝 **Use this space to make some notes**

....

....

....

....

....

....

2.3 | Stakeholder management

By completing this sub-section you will be able to:

■ define stakeholders and stakeholder management and explain why stakeholder analysis is important.

Stakeholders and stakeholder management

Definition – stakeholder

'The organisations or people who have an interest or role in the project, programme or portfolio, or are impacted by it.'

APM Body of Knowledge 6th edition

Definition – stakeholder management

'Stakeholder management is the systematic identification, analysis, planning and implementation of actions designed to engage with stakeholders.'

APM Body of Knowledge 6th edition

Stakeholder management process

Different stakeholders may clearly have differing views about the project and may support it or otherwise. They may have an opportunity to exert influence over the project in a positive or negative manner and there may be some influential stakeholders who may not want a project to go ahead. History is littered with projects that have failed to understand the magnitude of hostility towards their project or indeed the wave of enthusiasm and support that could have been tapped. Just think of the major road projects and the potential for pressure groups and lobbyists to blockade the route and interfere with their completion. A project manager must make sure that they identify all relevant stakeholders and thereafter endeavour to influence them to be positive towards it where possible.

The identification alone of stakeholders is not all there is, of course. They will need to be pro-actively managed throughout the project and typically the project manager will write this process down in a stakeholder management plan (or, typically, a communications plan). A suggested process for managing stakeholders appears below:

Table 2.2 Stakeholder management process

Identify stakeholders	We need to come up with a way of identifying stakeholders. If you work in a well-understood organisation and have been there for some time, you may well have come into contact with all the existing stakeholders. Teleport yourself to a new project with a new customer and you might need to start from scratch.
	Company organisation charts, websites, interviewing people, brainstorming sessions, talking to peers and colleagues, and generally working the system will reveal a whole host of people who may or may not have power and/or influence over what happens on your project.
	Typical types of stakeholders can include:
	■ individuals performing the project work;
	■ individuals and groups affected by the project work;
	■ owners, shareholders and customers;
	■ statutory and regulatory bodies.
Assess their interest and influence	Having got a list of the stakeholders, your next challenge is to understand which ones are important. This is normally done using a matrix, which estimates stakeholder interest and influence on the project outcome. This can be a simple scale using low/medium/high.

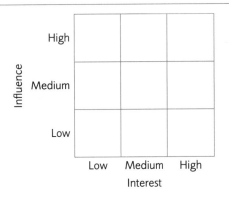

Figure 2.4 A stakeholder management grid

In addition, it can be useful to identify those stakeholders with a direct ability to affect the output and benefits. These are referred to as key stakeholders.

The principle is that you should be able to identify who the influential people are and place them in their relative positions. The process is quite subjective and a personal view – people change their attitudes over time, and the grid implies a fairly mechanical approach, while people are not really amenable to being categorised in this manner. When completing this analysis, project managers need to think about some key questions:

1. How will the project affect each of the stakeholders?

2. Will the stakeholders be supporting, negative or ambivalent about the project?

3. What expectations do the stakeholders have, and how can these be managed?

4. Who or what can influence the stakeholders' views about the project; are they affected by the attitudes of other stakeholders?

5. What would be the best way to engage with each of the stakeholders, and who is best placed to do it?

Develop communication plan	There may be issues that get in the way when we are trying to influence people. These can include the fact that: ■ they might not want to be influenced; ■ they might not want to exert any power to help or hinder anyway; ■ they might have a completely different attitude to the one you have anticipated;

	■ people change over time;
	■ being able to influence them may come at a price;
	■ you may need some help (to influence them).
	One of the key documents for any project is a communications management plan or a stakeholder management strategy to help guide your thinking and to document and substantiate your actions. The project manager is well advised to write one of these and include it as part of the PMP.
Engage and influence stakeholders	Here we need to a) enact the communication plans, and b) make sure our communication plans have worked. So we need to ensure that the planned actions have happened, and, if they didn't work, we need to do something different. You can use the stakeholder grid to re-assess their attitudes and position on a regular basis to determine trends and how effective you have been. This means that the stakeholder management plan is a dynamic document that must link to the other plans in the project management plan.
	Because of the wide variety of stakeholders there are no 'silver bullet' recommendations here but active engagement can include:
	■ meetings, one-to-one or group;
	■ newsletters, email circulars, posters;
	■ lobbying directly or through others;
	■ using incentives to encourage people to support the project;
	■ dealing with hurdles and solving problems that are perceived as such by stakeholders and participating in providing them with value from the project;
	■ implementing feedback processes to determine the perceptions of stakeholders;
	■ using the sponsor or project board to help influence more senior individuals.

Quick quiz (answers on pages 152–3)

	Question	Options	Your answer
1	What are the axes on a stakeholder analysis grid?	a) Power to affect the outcome of the project and influence over the successful delivery of the project	
		b) Power to affect the outcome of the project and interest in the delivery and outcome of the project	
		c) Power to affect the outcome of the project and control over the success of the project	
		d) Interest in the delivery of the outcome and influence over the success of the project	
2	Which of these is NOT a stage in stakeholder management?	a) Manage the engagement with the key stakeholders	
		b) Promote the interests of the key stakeholders	
		c) Identify the key stakeholders	
		d) Assess the power and interest of the project stakeholders	
3	A definition of a stakeholder is…	a) The people who have an interest or role in the project, programme or portfolio, or are impacted by it	
		b) The organisations which have an interest or role in the project, programme or portfolio, or are impacted by it	
		c) The organisations or people who have an interest in the project, programme or portfolio, or are impacted by it	
		d) The organisations or people who have an interest or role in the project, programme or portfolio, or are impacted by it	

		Question	Options	Your answer
4		Which of these is NOT a difficulty with assessing a stakeholder's position on the stakeholder grid?	a) It can appear a fairly mechanical approach b) Interest and influence are the axis labels c) Assessment of power and influence can be very subjective d) People may change their views over time	
5		Understanding the culture and expectations of stakeholders on a project will be key to understanding which project manager to appoint. Which is the most appropriate approach?	a) The selection of a project manager should be made based on the stakeholder expectations and culture alone b) The selection of the project manager should take into account the stakeholder culture and expectations c) The selection of the project manager should not take into account stakeholder culture and expectations d) The selection of the project manager is not related to stakeholder culture and expectations	

BIKEWEB CASE STUDY

"All systems go," Jayne said, as she burst in on Colin's Friday afternoon, waving a copy of the bank email around like it was a million pound note.

"Really? That's fantastic," he replied. "Does Zak know?"

"Yes – I just texted him. And I had that stakeholder meeting set for this afternoon, so it's just as well we've got the money, really."

"Do you need me?"

"Oh, yes please – it won't take long. I've asked the others to come along, too."

Later, they were all sitting around the meeting room table and Jayne had some sticky notes in her hand. She gave them each 10 and asked them to write in thick pen the names of all the people or groups who had an interest in the project. She had to explain, but they all got it.

While they were doing that, she drew onto the large white board the two axes of the stakeholder grid and labelled them 'Interest' and 'Influence'.

She then asked them to stick each of their sticky notes onto the grid. Lottie went first and explained whom she had identified and why; then Karim did the same; then Dean, Colin, Yuri and, finally, Sue. By this time there were a lot of duplicates, so Jayne filtered out those, but they were still left with quite a few.

They argued about some of them, especially where Zak should appear. They then thought of the firm that was doing the web design (although they hadn't yet been appointed) and the bank (because they were interested in the cash collection transfers).

They pondered it in silence for a bit, then Yuri said: "So now what, Mrs Project Manager?"

"Now we have to think about how we deal with them, and I will write that up so we all know what's going on and who's dealing with whom."

"Why do we need to write it down – pretty obvious, isn't it, no?"

"We need to make sure our message is clear. The really important stakeholders are the customers – we must ensure when we do the migration that, if there are problems, they don't get so fed up that we lose them all."

"So that's my job, I guess," said Sue. "I need to know the plan, then, don't I – so I can produce some marketing material and notices if there is to be some disruption?"

"Yes – that's exactly it." said Jayne. "We need a brief communication plan so we don't drop the ball with any of our stakeholders.

To be continued...

FUNDAMENTALS

Learning exercise

Draw your own version of the stakeholder grid and populate it with the BikeWeb stakeholders.

Use this space to make some notes

2.4 | Communications

By completing this sub-section you will be able to:

- define communications;
- outline different media of communication and identify potential barriers to effective communication;
- identify ways to facilitate effective communication;
- define the contents of a communications plan;
- explain the benefits of a communications plan.

Definition – communication

'Communication is the means by which information or instructions are exchanged. Successful communication occurs when the received meaning is the same as the transmitted meaning.'

APM Body of Knowledge 6th edition

The principles of communication

Understanding the audience – any activity must consider the nature of the audience and how they may wish to receive information – not only the mechanics of it, but their own personal preferences. The plan should take into account the options for delivering messages in a different format to different individuals, while balancing that with the costs involved.

Types of media – the project has a number of channels available to it in order to disseminate and receive any information. The most common channels are the traditional written word (or, more usually, typed on computer and emailed). There are now a huge and growing number of options available to most organisations in the way they disseminate information. Obviously these include all of those mechanisms above, but also social networking sites, collaboration software, websites, podcasts and other more innovative ways of getting a message across.

Barriers to communication

The project manager must be aware of the potential barriers to communication and make allowances for them. We typically think of physical barriers, but there are also cultural and psychological ones.

Think about your own environment and how these barriers have got in the way of your own communications and what you did (or could have done) about them.

Table 2.3 Barriers to communication

Barrier	What can be done to overcome	If you witnessed it, what did you do?
Perception on the part of the receiver	Make the message clear and unambiguous so that the message is not open to mis-interpretation. Use plain language without too much jargon or technical language, if it can be avoided.	
The environment, noise, fumes, heat, etc.	Try to make sure that the environment is fit for purpose for the message you are trying to convey. If you are having a personal conversation, do not do it in an open office.	
People's own attitudes, prejudices and emotional state	Try to understand the person who will receive the information and be sympathetic to their needs. A logical argument in an emotional situation may not have the desired effect.	
Culture	Arising from a lack of a common understanding or differences across different disciplines.	
Time zones and geography	These days it is more common that the project manager will be dealing with people across the world. This introduces delays, unreasonable meeting times, etc. Try to get a regime that everyone can be comfortable with.	
Distractions and other priorities	Sometimes you will not appear as high up someone's list as you might like. Make life easy for them. Suggest options and offer to go to them; keep meetings short and frequent.	

How to facilitate effective communications

The project manager will need to make sure that they have a clear plan and execute it. There are a number of behavioural aspects to a project manager's role such as:

Openness and honesty – they should not disguise information in the mistaken belief that it will not matter.

Active listener – they should make sure they are engaged with the audience at all times and contribute positively when necessary. Effective communication is a two-way process.

Use appropriate media – as mentioned, they should ensure that they are engaging the audience in the most appropriate manner.

Seek feedback – the project manager should actively seek and encourage feedback both for themselves and the project generally. Communication is a two-way process and if you are continually in 'send mode' you will not be able to adapt the message to accommodate changes or pick up on the impact of barriers.

The role of the project communication plan

The project communication plan is a section of the main PMP (therefore owned by the project manager) and includes a number of key areas. Typical contents of the communication plan might include the following:

The potential audience for the communication. The work done on stakeholder analysis in the start-up phases will be vital in identifying who the project needs to communicate with and seek to influence. The stakeholder analysis helps to prioritise our communication efforts and should be updated as the project progresses, so that the changes in the attitude of stakeholders to the project can be mapped. This enables us to demonstrate the effectiveness of the communication strategy.

What communication will be undertaken? The plan will describe the information that needs to be communicated into and out of the project. This may include reports and other formal documents on a regular basis and also describe what informal information needs to be disseminated and when.

When will the communication be undertaken? For example, is there to be a monthly briefing, when will the newsletters come out, how frequent will be team meetings, etc.

How will communication be undertaken? The plan must have a clear strategy for the various communication channels available. These fall into the following main categories of communication:

- **Formal verbal** – includes such things as meetings, interviews, presentations, briefings etc. They may be formal phase gate reviews, team meetings, stakeholder briefings etc. They are recorded in minutes or by other means so they can be referenced if required.

- **Informal verbal** – includes water cooler conversations, unrecorded telephone conversations etc. It is exceptionally difficult to script these types of communication, but some organisations will give their staff a large amount of training to deal with press interviews, for example, so it is possible. Good practice dictates that any verbal communication be followed up with a written record.

- **Formal written** — includes reports, presentations, minutes, specifications, designs etc. They are anything planned to be produced and which is a fundamental component of the project. Their production is planned and intended to be formal.

- **Informal written** – includes sticky notes, email (although this is very often considered formal), blogs, forums etc. If an individual takes action based on informal information it can be a good indicator as to whether it is in fact informal or not. Leave a note on someone's desk to meet you for a meeting at two o'clock, and they will probably go. Is this formal or informal?

- **Non-verbal** – this type of communication relates to how individuals convey messages directly one-to-one or one-to-many. They are related to our own personal mannerisms and

our way of deporting ourselves, which is usually referred to as body language. The main principle is that our body language cannot be denied and will often convey more of the message than the words spoken or written.

- **Active communications** – this type of communication means going out and engaging with stakeholders using meetings, training, presentations and discussions. The benefit of this approach is that we can check understanding and it provides opportunities to ask questions. For example, in our BikeWeb project, we can arrange training for the customer support team on the features of the new website and how to fix customer problems.

- **Passive communications** – this type of communication involves providing information to stakeholders so they can access it when they need it. This includes leaflets, manuals, websites, newsletters and even email. This can be more effective at communicating with a large stakeholder group, such as the customers of BikeWeb, but it presents less opportunity to check understanding and ask questions.

In all cases, we anticipate that the recipient will take some action based upon the communication, and a measure of its effectiveness will be whether they understand and whether their attitudes, behaviours or actions do actually change as a result. Informal communication is more difficult to manage and dependent upon the culture and networks existing in the organisation and, being unplanned, it can happen anytime.

Costs – communication costs money. The type and volume of communication is largely dependent upon the resources required to deliver it. Face-to-face meetings are valuable, but can be terribly expensive, especially if long-distance travel is involved. Each of the activities associated with communication on the project will need to be included in the scope and therefore costed into the budgets.

Feedback – know how feedback will be collected and what will be done as a result.

Benefits of a communication plan

If communication planning and execution are badly managed, a number of adverse consequences may occur. By producing a plan, the project manager can ensure that both individuals and groups are engaged in the most effective manner. Costs will be saved, as there will be less wasted time and energy correcting miscommunication. The people that can help will be identified and engaged early on and anyone who may have a negative influence can be properly attended to.

Quick quiz (answers on pages 153–4)

	Question	Options	Your answer
1	Who owns and manages the communication plan?	a) The project management team members b) The project sponsor c) The users of the project outputs d) The project manager	
2	Which of the following statements relating to the communication plan is true?	a) The communication plan is a key part of the project business case b) The communication plan is recorded as part of the issue log for the project c) The communication plan is part of the project management plan d) The communication plan is integral to the project risk log	
3	How do you know if communication has been successful?	a) The effectiveness of project communication cannot be measured b) It is possible to measure the effectiveness of project communications from the perception of the project sponsor c) The effectiveness of project communication can be measured by evaluating feedback from the key stakeholders d) The effectiveness of project communication can be evaluated by evaluating how much has been spent	
4	Which of these is NOT an example of a barrier to communication?	a) The environment b) Prejudice c) Attitudes d) Planning	
5	The making of hand gestures when speaking is an example of what?	a) Paralingual b) Emotional c) Body language d) Monotone	

BIKEWEB CASE STUDY

They all worked for another hour, making notes about who would do what and who would deal with the various stakeholders. They had already agreed that the project board should be Jayne, Colin and Zak. Sue, from marketing, would be accountable for the communications to the customers and she would actually be their voice when it came to the design. She had a really good idea of what they all wanted, and what would work and what wouldn't.

Karim would be the technical contact with whoever the web designers turned out to be, and Jayne would deal with the bank.

Lottie, Dean and Yuri would continue to deal direct with the digitising agency, and they would make sure that all the maps were ready. The plan wasn't ready yet, but Jayne left for the weekend with a spring in her step. The team seemed quite positive – even Yuri ended up sounding more cheerful.

Next week the planning would start in earnest, and Jayne would have a draft project management plan, including the outcome from the afternoon's meeting, ready for an inaugural project board next Friday.

To be continued...

Use this space to make some notes

3 Definition

3.1 The project management plan

By completing this sub-section, you will be able to:

■ state the main purpose of the project management plan;

■ define who is involved in the creation of the project management plan;

■ outline the contents of a project management plan;

■ explain why the project management plan needs to be approved, owned and shared.

Why do we need a project management plan?

We have already introduced the idea of a project management plan, but we now need to look at it in a bit more detail to make sure that its authorship and purpose are clear. A project management plan is a document that can be used by everyone to help:

■ explain the nature of the project. Describe its scope, the deliverables, timescales and roles and responsibilities;

■ explain the policy, procedures and processes that will be used to run the project. For example, how the project manager will make sure risks are being dealt with appropriately through the use of a risk management plan. Please note that this may well be a section in the main PMP rather than a separate document, or risks can be set out in separate documents, sometimes called a strategy, e.g. procurement strategy;

■ communicate these various strategies and plans to a wider audience. The document needs to be a working document – its contents are used to inform stakeholders and it must be kept up to date;

■ provide a baseline from which further measurement and analysis of variations can take place. When tasks on the project are underway, their actual durations and the expenditure will be compared with the PMP to ensure they are going in the right direction;

■ act as a sort of 'contract' between the project manager and the project sponsor. It describes what the sponsor is expecting the project manager to deliver. It may also have a role if you were a supplier to a client, in which case the PMP would serve the same purpose, except in this case it would probably form part of an actual, legally-binding contract;

■ provide a mechanism for continuity throughout the project life cycle. There is no guarantee of continuity of staff, and the PMP provides the single document that makes it possible to ensure that all the information necessary to run the project is available and up to date.

Who writes a PMP?

The project manager will take the business case and, under the authority of the sponsor, write the PMP. In a lot of cases, they will not need to write it from scratch – they may use one from somewhere else as a guide; there may be organisational rules as to how they are created along with blank templates; and they may be able to use other people to do a lot of the actual drafting.

Whatever happens, after a relatively short period (relative to the size and complexity of the project) they will produce the completed document to answer all the questions identified below. It is then reviewed by the sponsor. The sponsor will need to ensure that it does, in fact, conform to the business case and that its predictions of time and money are in line with the requirements of the business case.

In writing the PMP, the project manager may require specialist input from suppliers (for accurate prices), from subject matter experts (such as risk analysts and accountants), and perhaps from the team members, to make sure that the proposals are deliverable. It is a cardinal error to write a PMP in isolation and simply hand it over for the team to follow, as they will not feel engaged in it or inclined to follow it.

Contents of a PMP

The PMP is divided into two parts.

Policy level – This section sets out the principles for the management of the project, for example, the procedures to control change, project risk or quality. It describes the steps we will take to control scope change during the project or communicate with stakeholders. It includes copies of templates and forms that need to be completed at each stage of the process.

In most organisations, you will find that these processes and procedures are common across the organisation.

Delivery level – The delivery level documents describe how the project work will be done.

This section basically falls into the categories of:

Table 3.1 PMP contents

WHY (are we doing the project?)	The project management plan is built on the work done in the project business case. The underlying reasons for doing the project will be reproduced or referenced from the business case. These need not be rewritten but can simply be referenced and include: ■ description of benefits; ■ statement of requirements; ■ project objectives (for the chosen project).
WHEN (are we doing the project?)	The project schedule is a key document within a PMP. This may be limited to a high-level summary Gantt chart of the key milestones and stages but will usually be a fairly detailed document supported by a range of other scheduling information. Specific contents include: ■ precedence diagrams; ■ Gantt charts; ■ project life cycle; ■ milestones.
WHAT (will the project produce?)	This section describes the nature of the project deliverables created to satisfy the project requirements and organisation needs. Particularly, it helps to describe the: ■ scope of the project, including being specific about what is included and excluded; ■ product specifications for each of the main products to be delivered by the project; ■ acceptance criteria, which define how the 'customer' will approve the deliverables; ■ key performance measures, which define how the project's performance will be measured during delivery; ■ constraints, such as critical time slots or limitations on resources; ■ assumptions on which the plan has been formulated, such as the availability of access to a system or site to complete the project.

FUNDAMENTALS

HOW (will the project be run? Its processes.)	This section describes the approach to the delivery of the project. This can include the technology to be adopted and the stages the project may be broken into. Maybe you plan to run a pilot project first before rolling it out across the user community. This section would also describe the procurement approach – what will be done in-house and what will be procured externally.
WHO (will be involved and what will they be responsible for?)	This section contains the various roles, people, skills, reporting lines, accountability and engagement with the staff who will deliver the project. It is not in itself a list of the stakeholders, but a stakeholder analysis will help when putting this together. It also helps to include (all of which are detailed later in this guide): ■ a responsibility assignment matrix, which defines who is responsible for the completion of each product; ■ an organisational breakdown structure, which shows the organisational hierarchy for the project; ■ role descriptions, which clearly define the overall responsibilities within the project; ■ resources required to deliver the project.
WHERE (will the project take place and what logistical arrangements are needed?)	The project may involve various geographies, and locations of staff, offices, customers and suppliers all need to be considered, especially in the instance of multiple cultures and diverse nationalities. Hence the contents of this section might include: ■ environmental issues, including how waste will be minimised and how reuse and recycling will be encouraged; ■ communication planning, which needs to take account of any remote locations and how communications will be maintained.
HOW MUCH (will the project cost? Its budget.)	This section summarises the project budget, cash flow, the mechanisms for cost management and how variances are to be dealt with. Being able to predict with some certainty the rate at which the project will be spending its funds is crucial to knowing whether the project is on track or not. It will include (all of which are detailed later in this guide): ■ budget, including a time phasing, which shows when the funding will be required; ■ earned value arrangements for tracking actual cost and progress against the plan; ■ variation actions, describing the procedures for agreeing changes in cost; ■ cost management procedures, including procedures for reviewing the estimated costs and maintaining up-to-date forecasts.

The PMP is finalised at the end of the definition phase of the project but will usually have been created much earlier and continually revised over time until it is approved.

Why does a PMP need to be shared?

We saw earlier in the communications section how important it is to ensure regular and consistent feedback. The PMP is a kind of user manual for the project. Everyone on the team, and in fact all stakeholders, need a common understanding of the project, so they all need access to the project management plan. (In practice, some parts of the plan may be commercially sensitive or not relevant to all stakeholders, so some of them may need an edited form of the PMP. Particularly, it will contain the processes that are to be followed to ensure a quality result. If the project has an audit, the auditors may want to see evidence that the processes are being followed. If people are unaware of its contents, they will be unlikely to follow the processes set out in it.

 Quick quiz (answers on page 154)

	Question	Options	Your answer
1	Which statement best describes the ownership of the project management plan?	a) The project sponsor owns the project management plan but it should be developed with the project manager b) The project manager owns the project management plan but it should be developed with the wider team c) The organisation owns the project management plan but it should be written by the project manage d) The project office owns the project management plan but it should be developed with the project manager	
2	Which of these is NOT contained in the project management plan?	a) The investment appraisal for the project b) The risk management plan, which describes the way in which the project risk will be managed c) The project objectives, including a statement of the business problem or opportunity d) The success criteria against which the project will be evaluated	

FUNDAMENTALS

	Question	Options	Your answer
3	Changes to the project management plan are approved by...	a) The project manager b) The procurement department c) The users d) The project sponsor	
4	A policy level plan is...	a) A set of plans that describe the task to be completed to complete the project deliverable b) A company policy that is of little relevance to the delivery of the project c) A series of plans that set out the principles for how each aspect of the work will be managed d) Developed by the project manager in isolation from the rest of the projects in the organisation	
5	Once the PMP is agreed, it is shared with...	a) The project manager and the sponsor b) The project manager, users and sponsor c) All stakeholders d) Anybody with a direct involvement with the project	

BIKEWEB CASE STUDY

Jayne had nearly finished the PMP. Most of the main components were in there, but she didn't yet have a plan of when things would happen. She had asked Colin and Karim to help her out, and they had agreed to spare a bit of time later in the week. In the meantime, Jayne had ordered a new piece of planning software and was hoping to use this to speed things up. It had been really drummed into her on the course that she needed to build a plan with input from others rather than trying to do it all on her own, and that software was not the whole solution for a decent plan.

The PMP was about 12 pages long and she needed to present it to Zak and Colin properly on Friday. As it was the main document for the project they needed to agree everything in it. It might take a week more to get it finished, but she was quietly confident, although still a bit nervous that they would see it as useless bureaucracy. She was under pressure to get going now, and had already started doing some of the project preparatory work before getting the plan approved. She recognised that this was a risk, but the PMP would be ready soon, she was well underway now and had to carry on with the principles of project management. She liked the structure it brought and was confident it would help her deliver the project on time.

To be continued...

Learning exercise

Who do you think ought to be reading Jayne's project management plan? Who should have a copy?

FUNDAMENTALS

![pencil icon] **Use this space to make some notes**

....

....

....

....

....

....

....

3.2 | Scope management

By completing this sub-section you will be able to:

■ define project scope management;

■ describe how product breakdown and work breakdown structures are used to illustrate the scope of work required;

■ define the use of cost breakdown and organisational breakdown structures and RAM charts.

What is the 'scope' of a project?

We saw in Section 1 when discussing the project balance that the scope of a project is everything the project will do and everything it will produce. It is also useful to define what is outside of scope to avoid misunderstandings. Clearly defining what is in and out of scope reduces risk and manages the expectations of all key stakeholders.

In some cases the term 'scope' can be extended to include the benefits. This is especially true in the early stages of the project. For example, a project may set out to increase the number of subscribers to a website like BikeWeb. Remember, the business case is constructed to identify options to capitalise on opportunities or deal with problems. The subsequent project will be described in the business case in high-level terms, with phrases such as:

■ the project will build three new buildings;

■ the project will launch the products in Thailand and Indonesia;

■ the scope includes the design, build and test stages, but not roll-out.

This is fine as far as it goes, but it is obvious that these statements will be inadequate once the real planning is underway, as the detail is simply not there.

Describe how the PBS and WBS assist in understanding the work required

As the project definition progresses, the PMP requires ever more detailed refinement of the scope, so that there is evidence for the exact nature of the deliverables. Detailed scope is developed by creating a work breakdown structure (WBS) and a product breakdown structure (PBS).

It is important to keep the business case in mind, so that the PMP does not diverge from it and to make sure that the resultant project does in fact adhere, in principle and in practice, to the requirements set out in it.

It is these two key components (PBS – products and WBS – work) that help us develop the eventual plans and schedules that we need to be able to manage the project properly. It can be helpful to think of the WBS and PBS as two sides of the same coin. One describes the work required (to produce the products) and the other describes what will be produced (as a result of the work). Very simplistically, the WBS is a diagrammatic way of conveying the structure of the project (see diagram in Figure 3.1) which is used to define the hierarchical breakdown of work required to deliver the products of a project. Major categories are broken down into smaller components. These are sub-divided until the lowest required level of detail is established. The lowest units of the WBS become the activities in a project. The WBS defines the total work to be undertaken on the project and provides a structure for all subsequent project monitoring. For example, during the project we would want to establish how much time had been booked against a certain task to work out how far through it was.

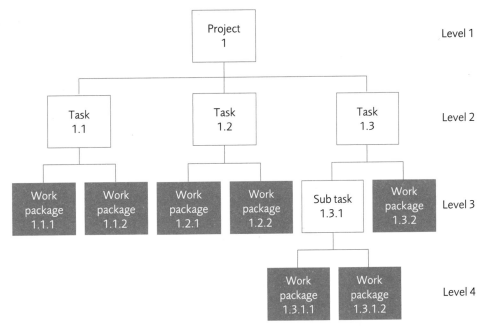

Figure 3.1 A work breakdown structure (WBS)

There are a few key components to recognise in a WBS:

- Each level is clearly identified (through the numbering structure) as being a breakdown of the level above (1.1.n. etc.).

- The levels start at 1 and develop as the level of detail increases.

- The lowest level (work) in the structure is called a work package(s).

- Each work package can consist of a number of activities, where it is required to plan at this level of detail. It is normally the lowest level of work package that will appear in the later Gantt charts.

- There are no predetermined numbers of levels – it is a judgement that must be made for each set of circumstances.

- The activities must include project management, as this is a component of the project work and must therefore appear in the WBS.

- The WBS includes everything that is in (and therefore, by definition, everything that is outside) scope.

Similarly, work packages have some specific characteristics:

- They are the smallest indivisible unit of work for which a budget is estimated and reported. There can be different levels (as above) and each is a breakdown of the one above.

- They should be able to have a discrete estimate associated with them so that proper recording can be maintained for any lessons learned.

- They have a discrete budget allocated to them, so their eventual cost can be accurately compared with the budget.

- They should be allocated to a single responsible person, to avoid confusion.

- They should not overlap, each containing a discrete, self-contained parcel of work.

- They should have some form of consistent numbering to identify them.

- Each work package either has a relatively short duration, or can be divided into a series of activities whose status can be objectively measured.

- They can be further broken down if that detail is required.

You will notice that there is very little difference in practice between a PBS and WBS from a diagrammatic point of view. The main points to note are that the WBS talks about work and will use verbs, while the PBS talks about products and will therefore use nouns. You can use either as the primary breakdown and may want to do both. Quite often your organisation will have a stated preference and will dictate how these breakdowns are constructed and, indeed, which type to use.

One key advantage of the PBS is that it gives you a definitive list of interrelated products that will prove invaluable when you come to do configuration management, as it will form the backbone of the configuration library. We will, however, from now on consider only the WBS rather than the PBS technique.

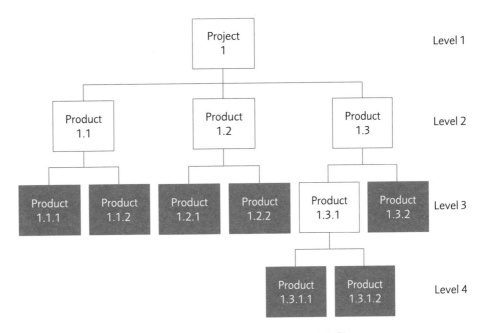

Figure 3.2 A product breakdown structure (PBS)

Define cost breakdown structures, organisation breakdown structures and RAM charts

Once again, the general basic theme of breaking things down is followed, in that the higher levels get decomposed to lower sub-levels. In the case of a cost breakdown structure, we are seeking now to break the overall project costs down into component parts; in Figure 3.3 these are simply labour, materials and overheads. In a large project being run by a company with sophisticated accounting systems, the project accountants will be able to use these to

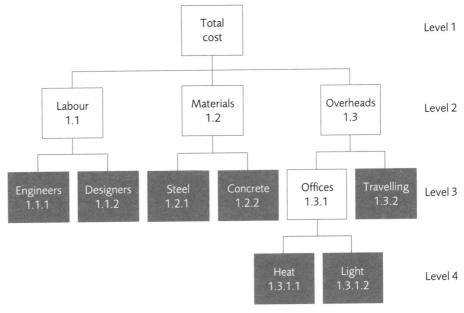

Figure 3.3 A cost breakdown structure (CBS)

FUNDAMENTALS

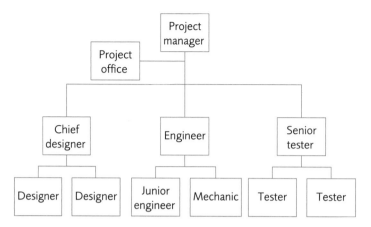

Figure 3.4 **An organisation breakdown structure (OBS)**

help account accurately for the costs of the project. In the diagram, it would be possible, for example, to see how much labour had been spent overall.

Figure 3.4 shows yet another breakdown diagram, this time one for the project organisation. There are a few key components to recognise in an organisation breakdown structure (OBS):

■ Each person who has a role in the project should be identified in the OBS.

■ It is not merely a 'cut-and-paste' from the company's organisation chart; careful thought will be needed.

■ The OBS demonstrates the communications and reporting links for the project; it does not necessarily represent line management roles.

■ Each role ought to have either a role description, terms of reference, statement of work, or some other mechanism to clearly identify what is required of the individual.

The primary use of the organisational breakdown structure is to be able to communicate to stakeholders the relevant individuals associated with the project. However, the real power of the OBS comes when it is combined with the WBS to provide a matrix of roles called a responsibility assignment matrix (RAM) or RACI chart.

As you can see, the roles described in the OBS (on the right) map across to the WBS (from the top). At the intersection we describe one of four possible characteristics of the individual (from the OBS) and the work (from the WBS) in the following way:

R – Responsible. This is the person who is responsible for carrying out the task; the person who will do it. Only one person should be responsible for the task.

A – Accountable. This is the individual or organisation that is accountable for getting the job done. They may make an individual or organisation responsible (to them).

C – Consulted. These are the individuals who are consulted in the execution of the task.

I – Informed. These are the individuals or organisations that are informed about the activity and provided with the output.

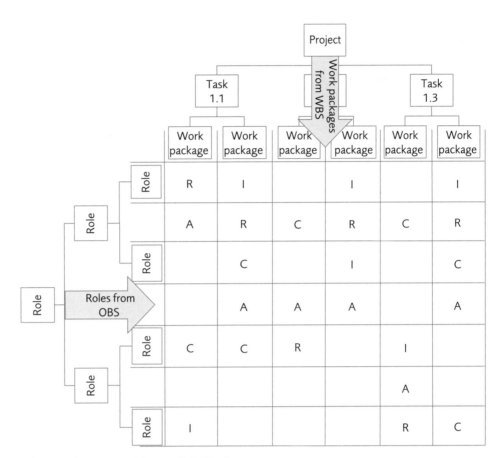

Figure 3.5 A RAM or RACI chart

Because of the naming convention adopted above, these RAM charts are sometimes referred to as RACI charts. The real benefit of them is that, at a glance, it is possible to identify who is doing what. There should be no missing responsibilities and likewise there should not be more than one individual/group responsible for any one task. It is a very powerful tool for the project manager and is a key component of the PMP.

 Quick quiz (answers on pages 154–5)

	Question	Options	Your answer
1	OBS means...	a) Outline breakdown structure	
		b) Organisation benefits structure	
		c) Organisation breakdown structure	
		d) Organisational benefits system	

FUNDAMENTALS

	Question	Options	Your answer
2	WBS means...	a) Work benefit system b) Work baseline system c) Work bottom system d) Work breakdown structure	
3	Each level of the WBS will be easily identifiable as a sub-level of the level...	a) Below b) Beside c) Above d) Behind	
4	Scope is defined as...	a) All the products to be produced by the project b) Including outputs, but may be extended to cover benefits c) A summary of the benefits a project will produce and its associated costs d) All the work required to complete the project	
5	A RAM chart shows what?	a) The work package and when it will take place b) The work package and the person involved in it c) The person involved in a work package and when it will take place d) The risks associated with the work package	

BIKEWEB CASE STUDY

"So, Yuri, this is the work package for the loading of the data onto the mapping database. As you are the most senior of the three analysts, it's your job to look after this work package, so I have put you as the responsible person, and I have tried to be as clear as I can about what the output will be from all your hard work."

"So you have just written down what I'm already doing," he replied in his usual blunt way.

"Well, yes, in a way, but the really important bit is the estimate of time, which I need from you, and also a very clear description of what you will have done, what the database will look like, its acceptance criteria, so that we can all be sure that it is suitable."

"Of course it will be suitable," he said, sounding a bit irritated.

"But we need to know exactly that it has been done, tested, catalogued and indexed according to the standards here in the quality section of the PMP."

"Well, you wrote that – we do know what we are doing."

"OK, so that will be fine, then. So long as they are all indexed correctly, the web designers can pick them all up in their front-end so they can be merged when a customer buys more than one."

"I didn't know you wanted to do that."

"Do what?"

"Merge them when they buy more than one."

"I would have thought that would be something they will want to do, don't you?"

"Well, now you mention it, yes – I had better go and check a few things out. I hadn't allowed for it in the estimates I've given you."

Jayne looked at him blankly and said: "OK, so go and check that out, then. We need to see what other bits of the mapping need to be sorted out. What other assumptions have you been making?"

The planning seemed to be paying dividends. This would have been a big problem later.

To be continued...

Learning exercise

Write down here what you think are the main elements of the BikeWeb project scope – what is included in the project?

3.3 | # Estimating

By completing this sub-section you will be able to:

- describe the estimating funnel;

- identify typical estimating methods (including analytical, comparative, parametric).

Estimating accuracy and the estimating funnel

There are significant problems when we are asked to come up with an estimate. How long will it take to do this or that presents quite a difficulty, especially if it has never been done before. The only real truth is that you only really know exactly how long something is going to take to do just after you have finished doing it. Project managers, though, are likely to get two questions asked of them fairly frequently – how much is the project going to cost and when will it be finished?

The diagram below shows that our ability to estimate accurately improves as we get further into the project. At the very start of even thinking about the project, the estimates will be either very high above or very low below the final cost. Over time, the estimates evolve and gradually get closer to the final cost. At the beginning, we are significantly out from the eventual cost. At the end closer but there is still a difference. The principle is that our estimates improve over time as our uncertainty decreases – indicated by the curved lines.

Putting this into your own life, you may know what you are doing next weekend, but what you will be doing in four years' time will probably be much less well known.

The key factor in the accuracy of the estimate is our knowledge about the project, as represented by the bottom axis. By the time we commit to the project implementation, we ought to be in possession of more of the available information, and this will mean our estimates are greatly improved. This is only true, of course, if we continually refine the estimates.

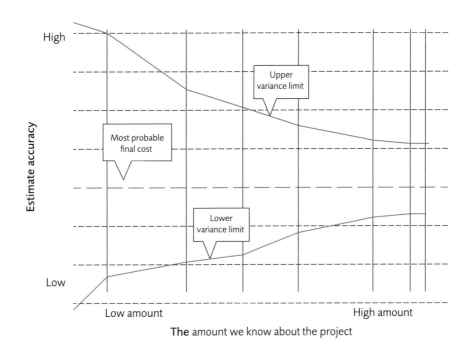

Figure 3.6 The way estimating accuracy improves over time

Estimating methods

Analytical estimating (also known as 'bottom-up')

If we know the component work packages for a project, which will have been developed using the work breakdown structure, we can build up a more thorough and detailed idea of the top-level cost by adding them up from the bottom.

This type of estimate relies on a very well-developed specification of the various components and is therefore not really possible during the early stages of a project. We can use the WBS from earlier to provide this lower level of detail as it becomes known.

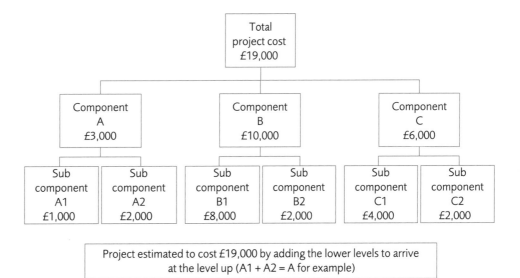

Figure 3.7 An example of bottom-up estimating

Comparative estimating (or analogous estimating)

A comparative estimate is where we take historical data from a similar project and simply scale it and make any allowances that we can to help arrive at a better value. The past costs are scaled by the scope and complexity to produce the estimate. For example, if a construction firm built a three-bedroomed house last month and it cost £100,000, when they come to build another next month, it will be approximately £100,000. They would then have to take into account any variables that have changed – for example, the cost of bricks may have increased, and so an adjustment may be needed.

Parametric estimating

This form of estimate relies on defined parameters against which the work can be measured, such as the area of a building or the number of users of a PC network. Using these numbers we can predict the total cost of the project. For example, if we wanted to produce 10 software modules and we knew that they take on average five days each, our estimate for them all would be 50 days. It is simple and quick. However, of course, the problems are that if there is a small error in the base data, it will cause significant errors later on. It also relies on a very well-developed body of data on which to draw, which would have been built up over a long period of time, and they must be representative of the job we are doing now.

We could not say that all of the modules would take five days – some would take four and others, six – but the parametric detail would work out in the end.

Learning exercise

BikeWeb

If you had to estimate how long it would take to upload the various maps and other content to the website, how would you do it?

Quick quiz (answers on page 156)

	Question	Options	Your answer
1	A _____ estimate will compare one project with another, similar project.	a) Parametric b) Bottom-up c) Comparative d) Guesstimate	
2	Which is the best description of a comparative estimate?	a) Comparative, or analogous, estimating uses historical data from similar projects or programmes to extrapolate estimates for new work b) A comparative estimate uses defined parameters by which work can be measured c) A comparative estimate uses a detailed specification to estimate time and cost for each component of the work d) A comparative estimate uses best case, worst case and mostly assessment	
3	What other technique is fundamental to the creation of a bottom-up estimate?	a) PBS b) OBS c) WBS d) Gantt chart	
4	Whom should the project manager consult in the creation of estimates?	a) The suppliers b) The users c) The sponsor d) All of the above	
5	Input to parametric estimates might NOT include what?	a) Price per tonne b) Man/day cost c) Mile of road d) PERT	

FUNDAMENTALS

BIKEWEB CASE STUDY

Yuri and Jayne had worked all the way through the main steps in the work he was doing and Jayne was busily scribbling all of that down to add to the work package definition. Yuri had not included the indexing work, so together they had arrived at a way of making sure that the data was indexed correctly.

They talked about how to estimate the remaining time and, as they had already done about 100 maps, they had some really good comparative data to use. From this, they worked out that it took about half a day to do each one. The entire catalogue was just over 1,000 maps, so they used a parametric estimate and multiplied the time for one map by the 900 left to do to get to 450 days.

"Wow – that seems a lot," Yuri looked genuinely surprised by that figure. "We will get quicker,"

"OK, but let's use that as a sort of worst case, and I will put it into the schedule."

"There are three of us," said Yuri.

"Yes, OK, so there is 450 days' work over 150 days."

"But that's 30 weeks!" said Yuri.

"You are going to be a busy boy, then," she grinned.

To be continued...

Use this space to make some notes

| 3.4 | **Scheduling** |

By completing this sub-section, you will be able to:

- identify the purpose of scheduling;
- outline different approaches to scheduling, including critical path analysis, total float, Gantt (bar) charts, baseline, milestone.

Definition – resource scheduling

'Resource scheduling is a collection of techniques used to calculate the resources required to deliver the work and when they will be required.'

APM Body of Knowledge 6th edition

Definition – time scheduling

'Time scheduling is a collection of techniques used to present schedules that show when work will be performed.'

APM Body of Knowledge 6th edition

Producing a project schedule

Most project managers can be recognised by the fact that they are clutching a Gantt chart. This has become the mainstay of project schedule production and it is usually created on a piece of computer software, of which there are hundreds of different kinds to choose from. If a project manager does not have a schedule of when things are expected to happen, they will not be able to predict sufficiently accurately when they might need staff, facilities, materials etc. Importantly, scheduling does not just apply to time scheduling but also resource scheduling.

The purposes of scheduling

The purposes of scheduling are to:

- determine the overall project duration and when activities ought to happen;
- predict the future and allow enough notice to start the project in time to meet the end date;

- forewarn and plan for other human resources and team members when they will be required by the project;

- book facilities and other non-human resources, such as testing facilities, and special equipment, such as cranes;

- make provision in the company for enough funds to be available to pay for the costs of the project;

- enable the project manager to communicate an overview of the timescales to the main stakeholders;

- help identify key milestones to describe where key events or deliverables will take place.

Approaches to scheduling

The following few diagrams go some of the way to describing how these Gantt charts are created. We have already discussed the creation of a work breakdown structure, and it is this that is the starting point for producing a schedule. It allows the project manager to understand all the work that needs to be done in order to deliver the project.

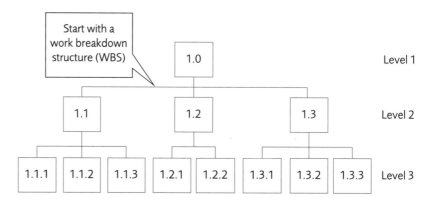

Figure 3.8 The creation of a precedence diagram from a work breakdown structure (1)

Once we have a work breakdown structure we can consider moving it on to generate a precedence diagram. The method for doing this is called the precedence diagram method (or PDM). Each of the lowest levels (work packages) are placed into a logical sequence, working from left to right. The arrows between the work package boxes indicate a relationship, and the normal relationship is that of finish-to-start, as in Figure 3.9. This is the most common way of linking tasks and will usually be sufficient for simple plans.

The connection implied here simply means that 1.1.2 cannot start until 1.1.1 has finished. This does not mean that it has to start immediately, but merely that it can be started. This

Figure 3.9 Finish-to-start relationship

point is quite important, as it means that, in theory, a gap in time can appear between the end of one task and the start of the next. This gap is referred to as 'float', which we will explore later.

So, utilising finish-to-start connections, we can start to 'hook up' all of the work packages to provide a complete picture of the end-to-end logic of the project. If all the connections are made, the project will appear as a diagram similar to the one shown in Figure 3.10. We have made some assumptions about this sequence, i.e., which work packages follow which. Don't worry that you are missing something here – it is only a demonstration of how the technique works.

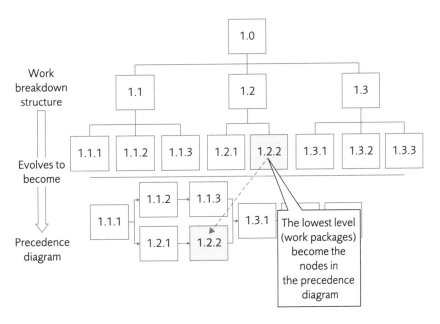

Figure 3.10 The creation of a precedence diagram from a work breakdown structure (2)

At the moment we have no durations on any of these work packages – this is the next step. Before we work on this, though, you will need to develop an understanding of a basic way of representing the scheduling data on a work package. This work package data has been described in a format as in Figure 3.11 which is widely recognised.

ES	D	EF
	Task ID	
LS	TF	LF

Key:

D is the duration

ES is the earliest that a task can start

EF is the earliest that a task can finish

LS is the latest that a task can start

LF is the latest that a task can finish

TF is the total float (discussed later)

Figure 3.11 Representing scheduling data

Precedence diagramming

If you apply these terms and complete a fully developed precedence diagram, you can build up a working knowledge of the earliest the project can finish, as well as a number of other key facts relating to the project, such as total float and the critical path through the precedence diagram.

So, we have taken the precedence diagram we created above and applied some fictitious durations to the work package nodes. By using those durations, we can produce an updated precedence diagram, as appears below in Figure 3.12. We need to assume that the relationships between the work package nodes have been clarified and are correct.

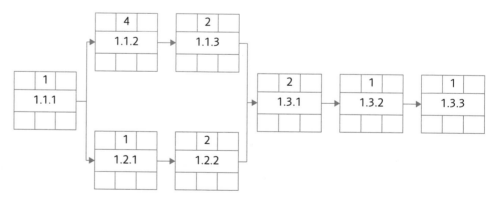

Figure 3.12 A basic precedence diagram to use as an example

Forward pass

In this example, the duration box (middle top of each work package node) has been completed. The first thing when calculating the critical path through the precedence diagram is to carry out a 'forward pass' through the diagram.

We do this by starting at the far left and populating the early start. Then we add the duration to calculate the early finish. In practical terms, think about a task that starts on Monday first thing. We know from our estimates that it should take one week, so the task should finish at end of business on the Friday. In our precedence diagram, we choose to start at week 0, add the one week of the task duration, and arrive at week 1 for the earliest finish.

If we apply this principle to the precedence diagram, we will end up with something like this (for the first node):

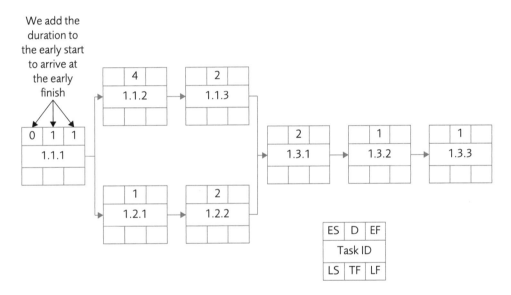

Figure 3.13 Precedence diagram showing early finish calculation

When we have done the first, we can continue with the forward pass and populate the top rows of all the work package nodes. There are two tricky bits.

■ The early finish from the predecessor work package node gets transposed into the early start in the subsequent node(s).

■ In the forward pass, if you have a choice about which number to take from the early finish to the early start, you always choose the higher number.

To move on, take a look at the next diagram. The shaded areas are the numbers we are worried about.

When you have finished adding all the way through, the last early finish box is the earliest date on which the project will finish. It is the sum of all the longer durations through the precedence diagram.

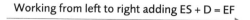

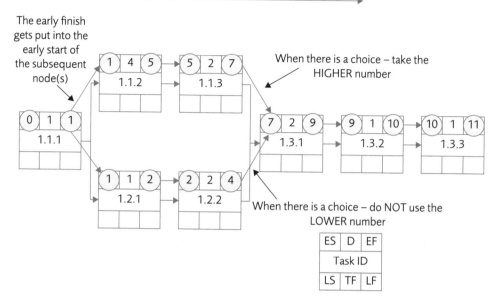

Figure 3.14 Precedence diagram showing early start and early finish calculations

Backward pass

The next job is to carry out the backward pass, Figure 3.15. Working from right to left, this time, we subtract the duration from the latest finish to arrive at the latest start. Again, there are a few tricky bits.

■ The latest start from the successor node gets entered into the latest finish for the predecessor node.

■ In the backward pass, if you have a choice about which number to take backwards from the latest start into the latest finish of the predecessor task, you always choose the lower number.

■ In the cases for the exam and to make life a bit easier in these examples, the earliest finish from the last node in the precedence diagram becomes the latest finish for that (last) work package node.

Total float and critical path

What the diagrams have shown so far is that, if we assume the latest finish is the same as the earliest finish and we work back from right to left, we get back to a zero as the latest start in the first node. This is correct for the purposes of the exam.

There is still a blank box in the middle on the bottom row of each of the work package nodes. This is reserved for the calculated total float. Total float is arrived at by subtracting the early finish from the latest finish of a given work package node. In the case of 1.1.3, Figure 3.15, this equals 0, as it does for most of the other work package nodes, except 1.2.1 and 1.2.2, which both have 3 in the total float box. Let's take a look at the finished diagram (Figure 3.16).

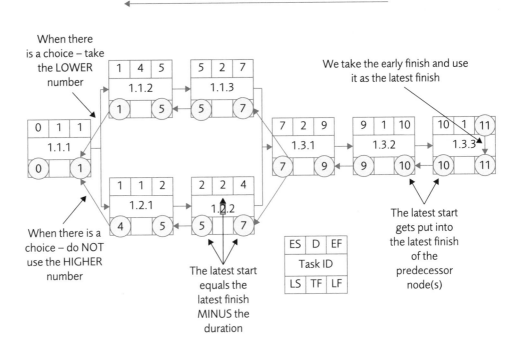

Figure 3.15 Precedence diagram showing latest start and finish calculations

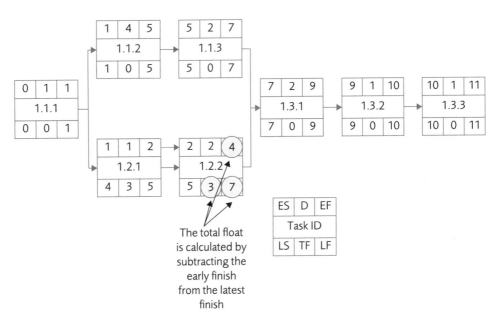

Figure 3.16 Precedence diagram showing total float calculations

The definition of the term 'total float' is "the amount of time by which a work package node can be delayed before it affects the end date of the project". In the diagram above, if 1.1.3 takes three weeks instead of two weeks, the end date will be delayed. This is because it has 0 weeks' total float, therefore no option to be lengthened or delayed.

In the diagram, if 1.2.2 is delayed by a week, it will not affect the end date, because it has three weeks' total float.

The critical path through the precedence diagram is that path that demonstrates the least total float. In the case of our example, it follows the path as defined in Figure 3.17. As can be seen the black lines on the diagram (the critical path) also show the longest duration through the project (11 weeks).

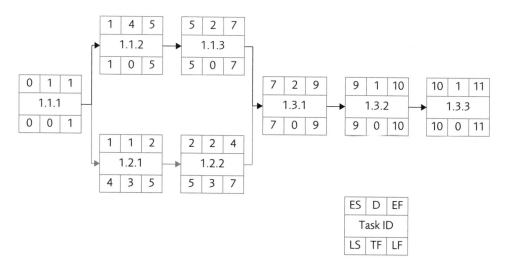

Figure 3.17 Precedence diagram showing the critical path

What is the point of the critical path?

Critical path analysis (as described in Figures 3.8 to 3.17) is the accepted method for calculating the optimal end date for a project. In doing so, it reveals the total float. This is important because:

■ tasks with the lowest combined total float describe the critical path. If we understand which tasks are going to affect the end date, we can pay a little more attention to them than some of the others. They are at the top of the project manager's list;

■ tasks that affect another task need to be understood, as their delay will affect another task and as such may need managerial intervention. They won't affect the end date of the project, though, and so are not as key as the ones with little or no total float;

■ tasks with total float have a degree of flexibility in their timings and therefore do not need to be as closely scrutinised and managed as the others. They may also represent those tasks that can have resources reduced to redeploy elsewhere, as extending them may not have ramifications for the end date;

■ by drawing the precedence diagram we are actively engaged in thinking about the detail of the interdependencies, the estimates, the relationships between tasks, the implications of delays and so on. If the team is engaged in the process the quality of the planning will improve dramatically.

Once the precedence diagrams have been produced, the next step is usually to convert them into a bar chart. The most common type is a Gantt chart, and this is the one most widely reproduced in planning software. The principle is quite simple. A Gantt chart has the tasks down the left hand axis and the timescale across the top, and the tasks are represented by a bar or line going from left to right, covering the start and end of that task. The migration of the precedence diagram to a Gantt chart is described in Figure 3.18.

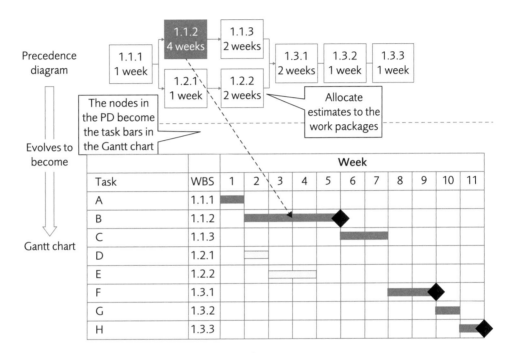

Figure 3.18 **The evolution of a precedence diagram into a Gantt chart**

Milestones and milestone slip charts

Simply showing bars on a chart can sometimes cause the really key events to become obscured. To solve this problem, there is an opportunity to highlight these points through the use of milestones. You can spot three milestones on the chart above (a milestone is usually demonstrated as a black diamond on the chart) and they have a number of key attributes in that each milestone:

■ represents a significant point in the project;

■ is a point, perhaps, where a contractor may be paid;

■ is a point, perhaps, where we may get paid;

■ is a high-level monitoring point with zero duration and no resources;

■ is a key deliverable.

Milestones should be interspersed throughout the project and used to monitor and control at a higher level than the detail of a Gantt chart or precedence diagram. A milestone is often chosen to represent the start of a new phase or completion of a major deliverable. They are used to monitor progress at summary level.

Baseline planning

Once the project plan has been produced, it is normal to nominate these initial dates and plans as being a baseline. The purpose of the baseline is to provide a 'line in the sand' – a point from which progress can be monitored and controlled. Any variation from the baseline will allow us to identify where any major deviation from the planned route has taken or may take place. In this way, the project manager can attempt to pull the project back on schedule through corrective actions.

Quick quiz (answers on page 157)

	Question	Options	Your answer
1	What is a visual representation of a project's planned activity against a calendar called?	a) A Gantt chart b) Critical path network c) A product flow diagram d) A Pareto chart	
2	Total float is the difference between latest finish and...	a) Early start b) Latest finish c) Early finish d) Free float	
3	For the precedence diagram below, what is the total duration of the project?	a) 20 days b) 18 days c) 28 days d) 5 days	
4	A milestone has what amount of time associated with it?	a) One day b) One week c) Zero d) All the float	

	Question	Options	Your answer
5	The critical path is the...	a) Sequence of activities through the precedence diagram from start to finish with the shortest durations	
		b) Sequence of activities through a precedence diagram from start to finish, the sum of whose durations determines the overall duration	
		c) Sequence of activities through a precedence diagram from start to finish, the difference between which determines float	
		d) Sequence of activities through a precedence diagram from start to finish, which determines the overall resource requirements	

BIKEWEB CASE STUDY

Jayne slowly worked through all of the jobs with the others and got an estimate for each. She then applied their figures to each task in her plan. When finished, she started putting them in order. She camped out in a small meeting room downstairs next to the stairwell and began piecing her project together as she had been taught.

After a while, though, she realised that she didn't really have enough information to complete the job on her own – she would need some more input from the team. For example, she wasn't sure if the hosting system for the website came all set up and ready to go, or whether there would be any configuring to do. And who in her team would be responsible for uploading the maps and data for the new site to the server and checking that it all worked? She was also worried about who was going to make sure the new payment system would work with the website.

Anyway, she prepared a draft plan on her own, entered it into a cheap charting package she had downloaded from the internet and printed it out in the form of a Gantt chart. She was quite pleased with the result and went back upstairs to her desk. Then, with a fresh cup of coffee, she set about checking all of her assumptions and the logic with the rest of the team. By the end of the day, the Gantt chart was on the wall beside her desk, alongside the stakeholder grid. She would check through it again in the morning and send it out as a draft plan for Colin and Zak to approve.

She went to the gym quite satisfied that she now had a plan and things would go well. She was confident of hitting the dates.

To be continued...

Learning exercise

What do you think the key dates are in the BikeWeb project? Where would you put Jayne's milestones?

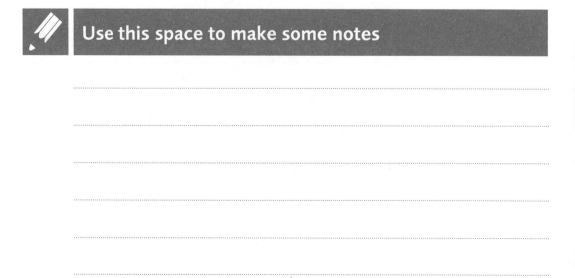

Use this space to make some notes

3.5 | Project resource management and procurement

By completing this sub-section you will be able to:

■ define procurement within the context of projects;

■ define resource management;

■ list different categories and types of resource needed for projects.

Procurement within projects

Definition – procurement

'Procurement is the process by which products and services are acquired from an external provider for incorporation into the project, programme or portfolio.'

APM Body of Knowledge 6th edition

What this means on a day-to-day basis is that most projects need to buy 'stuff'. This stuff can be standard, 'off the shelf' goods and services such as bricks or office accommodation, or goods or services that are designed and provided specifically for the purchaser, such as a kitchen or a marketing campaign or professional advice or consultancy such as public relations or design.

We have described below a very simple supplier selection process to illustrate the principles of how these acquisitions take place. There are usually a number of steps to go through, and most organisations will already have some rules and guidelines to help the project on its way. These procedures will almost certainly involve most of the following key stages:

Make or buy decision. The first thing to decide is if the organisation should do the work in-house or procure it from an external supplier. This is not as trivial as it seems, because it may depend upon the organisation's internal capabilities, resources and plans for the future.

The use of single, integrated or multiple providers. If the decision is taken to go outside the organisation, the next decision is how best to break up the project for procurement. It might be best to get everything done by one supplier, as this reduces interfaces that need to be managed. On the other hand, some projects benefit from having a number of different suppliers working on different parts.

Provider selection. Define the requirement that you need the supplier to meet and what you are expecting them to do, or the products you are expecting them to provide, and make sure that there is a suitable level of definition for the scope of work. Document it as part of the project documentation and record it in appropriate ways for later reference.

Issue an invitation to tender (ITT) to the various suppliers you would like a price from. This may follow an advertising process to determine who the likely suppliers might be. The ITT

FUNDAMENTALS

usually has a response period, and should include enough information for the potential bidders to respond. It should also include the criteria on which the responses will be judged, perhaps some form of compliance matrix where your key needs are valued and the suppliers scored against them. An ITT is sometimes referred to as an 'invitation to bid' or a 'request for quotation'.

Answer any queries raised by the bidder. It is normal to make sure that if one bidder asks a question, all the bidders see the answer. Sometime a bidder's conference can be held, where there is an interactive opportunity to ask questions and seek clarification.

Receive and evaluate bids and review against the compliance matrix. The bidders may well provide a lot of 'extras' over and above the specification and these can be considered, but straightforward compliance to the ITT is the minimum.

Award a contract to the successful bidder(s), making sure that the scope is as per the tender, bind in whatever documents are relevant and make sure that you and they fully understand the nature of the arrangement and their respective liabilities (what you and they have agreed to do).

Resource management

Definition – resource management

'Resource management comprises the acquisition and deployment of the internal and external resources required to deliver the project, programme or portfolio.'

APM Body of Knowledge 6th edition

Categories of resource

There are a number of types of resource to consider. Each will be treated differently by the project manager for the purpose of acquisition and deployment.

Consumable resources are those things that, once used, need to be replaced. Examples of these are fuel and money. The project manager must make appropriate arrangements for these to be replaced once used up. They do this by creating budgets and plans to ensure that all stakeholders are aware of the implications of their use, and what the consequences are when they are used up.

Re-usable resources can be redeployed when no longer needed – examples include people, accommodation, vehicles, etc. The project manager will need to make appropriate arrangements for the re-use of resources, especially the human ones. Care should be taken of any materiel that can be re-deployed to avoid scrappage costs and unnecessary expense.

Equipment used on the project needs to be allowed for. If a tunnel is being dug, a boring machine may be required. This is not a direct cost to the customer (we will not provide the machine at the end of the job) but we need it in order to fulfil the project activities.

Materials are used in the same way as equipment, except that they contribute directly towards the finished product. If we are building a new website, the artwork we purchase becomes a deliverable. These are direct costs associated with the creation of the website.

Space is usually required to house the project teams. For an IT project office, space will be required to accommodate the machines, people and support services.

 Quick quiz (answers on page 158)

	Question	Options	Your answer
1	Resource planning needs to be done when?	a) At the beginning b) At the end c) In the middle d) Over and over again as necessary	
2	Which of these is a type of resource?	a) Fixed b) Cost-based c) Re-usable d) Unused	
3	Which of these is an example of a re-usable resource?	a) Fuel b) People c) Money d) Time	
4	What does ITT stand for?	a) Intention to terminate b) Invitation to terminate c) Invitation to tender d) Innovative transfer time	
5	Against what would a supplier's tender be judged?	a) Tender form b) Project management plan c) Business case d) Compliance matrix	

FUNDAMENTALS

BIKEWEB CASE STUDY

Colin was flicking through the pack of information from the three web design suppliers. They had chosen to look at some alternatives as there had been some queries about the first one they had in mind when it came to the quality of their service.

"We need to get going on this,"

"According to the plan..." Jayne proudly waved it around, "we need to make a decision on who to go with by...let me see...yesterday."

"So how do we choose then?"

"I put a scoring matrix together," she pushed it across the desk to Colin and it looked like this.

COMPANY NAME	SCORES								
	Quality	Weight	Total	Price	Weight	Total	References	Weight	Total

WINNER IS...

Colin picked it up and said: "Well, those categories seem ok, Price, Quality and their References but they're not all as important as each other."

"That's what the weighting factor column is for," she replied. "We need to agree what the weighting factor is, then both of us in secret need to mark our scores (and I guess we ought to get Zak and Yuri to do the same), and then we multiply out all the scores and the top points wins."

"What if we don't get the answer we want?"

"Let's worry about that when the time comes."

To be continued...

Use this space to make some notes

....

....

....

....

....

....

3.6 | Risk management

By completing this sub-section you will be able to:

- define risk;
- define risk management;
- explain the purpose of risk management;
- outline a high-level risk management process;
- describe the use of a risk register.

What is a risk?

> **Definition – risk**
>
> 'The potential of an action or event to impact on the achievement of objectives.'
>
> *APM Body of Knowledge 6th edition*

The *APM Body of Knowledge* focuses attention on the overall impact of risk to the whole project outcome, including the benefits. This overall risk is made up of specific project risk events, such as 'possible failure of acceptance testing'.

It is important to differentiate between the causes of risks, the risk itself and the effect of a risk.

Take a simple example. There is a risk that we may not have enough of a specific resource for a critical stage in the project, such as commissioning or going live with BikeWeb's system. The causes of these risks are things like the fact that Karim is the only one who knows about the configuration of the bank payment interface, or the fact that Jayne is the only one trained in project management, or that the project relies on finance from the bank. These root causes create uncertainty (or risks) for the project, for example, Karim may not be able to get to work due to extreme weather, or Jayne may get a better job, or the bank may withdraw the funding. We are not sure these risks will happen; we might get lucky and none of these things might go wrong. However, if they do happen they have consequences (or effects) for the project; the project may become late or run out of money.

If the risk matures, there will be an impact, which we measure in terms of time, cost or failure to meet performance criteria.

There is a tendency to merely think of risks as threat-based (i.e. what might go wrong). APM encourages thought about the opposite (i.e. what might go right), and these are referred to as opportunities.

Benefits of a pro-active risk management process

A formal approach to risk management is intended to identify and pre-empt the things that might affect the project. Using a formal process allows thought and energy to be applied at the time it has the most value – at the beginning.

- The process will define the way in which risks are dealt with, the objectives and the roles of the various stakeholders.

- It encourages reflection on how things have gone – what worked, and what didn't stop problems occurring.

- It encourages thought about what to do if things do go wrong.

- It ensures that everyone is doing the same things in the same way.

- It provides a common reference point for any audit and assurance processes.

- It will make sure that the organisation enters into projects with a clear perspective of the risks, in the knowledge that all the avenues have been covered and problems ought to be fewer.

A risk management process

Definition – risk management

'Risk management is a process that allows individual risk events and overall risk to be understood and managed proactively, optimising success by minimising threats and maximising opportunities.'

APM Body of Knowledge 6th edition

A project needs to adopt a suitable and appropriate risk management process. A diagram of a simple one appears below. The diagram, although describing a relatively simple process, looks complicated because of all the arrows. These arrows around the boxes are significant, and imply that the steps are not isolated but are in fact iterative in a number of ways.

Following the process blindly is not going to be sufficient to manage risks effectively on the project. It is merely a framework around which the project manager and teams will need to use their skill, knowledge and ingenuity on an on-going basis to pre-empt the things that might interfere with the achievement of objectives. It must also be remembered that sometimes things may go better than planned and these instances are referred to as opportunities. Active management of opportunities will mean that the benefits derived from a project will be maximised.

Also, bear in mind that risk management does not include the management of things that have already occurred, which are referred to as issues (see later).

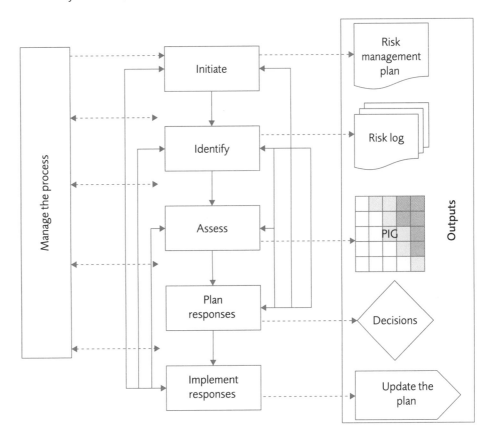

Figure 3.19 **The APM risk management process (annotated)**

The stages are discussed below.

Initiate

The main output from the initiation phase is the risk management plan. This document describes how risk will be managed and by whom. It simply describes the process that will be followed, and not responses to individual risks.

FUNDAMENTALS

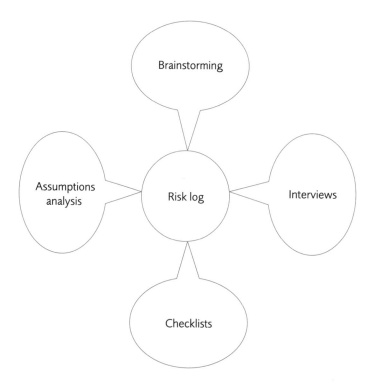

Figure 3.20 Risk identification techniques

Identify

During risk identification, the project manager is looking to identify the risk events that may affect the project. These events can be beneficial or detrimental. What this means is that the project manager should be looking out for things that may go better than planned as well as those that will be negative.

The key techniques for identifying risk, as set out in Figure 3.20, are described as follows:

- **Brainstorming** is the use of facilitated workshops to elicit 'blue sky' ideas from participants with a view to identifying risks that may be significant. Brainstorming gets a lot of good ideas out in the open quickly but, because of the number of people involved, it can be expensive and requires careful management.

- **Interviewing experts** involves calling on experts in the respective fields to help focus on specific components or activities in the project. Experts will tend to use their own, subjective perspective of what are risks and what are not. These views may differ from those of other 'experts'. They do yield a lot of valuable information though and help the project manager capitalise on experience.

- **Checklists** are widely used to help identify risks. They appear in all walks of life and stem from a systematic process done once to analyse potential areas of risk and deployed into repetitive situations to speed up the identification process. They are quick and relatively cheap, but sometimes doing the checklist can be perceived as doing the risk management, with the result that significant risks can be overlooked simply because they are not on the list.

■ **Assumptions analysis** is a mechanism of going through previous lists of assumptions and breaking them down to understand which risks may be a consequence of them. This is relatively quick and easy, and draws on work that has gone before. However, there is a danger in sticking only to the previous list of assumptions that some assumptions may be missed.

Assess

The most recognisable and common output from the risk assessment process is called the probability and impact grid (PIG), an example of which appears in Figure 3.21. The use of this example is to show that a risk is evaluated on two axes: that of probability (how likely it is to happen) and that of impact (what will happen if it does). The combination of these two factors is sometimes referred to as the risk severity.

In its most simple (and arguably most useful) form this grid can be used by the team to position individual risks against the two axes. This creates a visual and easily understood way of signifying which are more important to deal with. Clearly a very high (VHI) probability of a VHI risk would require the attention of the project manager first, whereas a very low (VLO)/VLO one can be left until later.

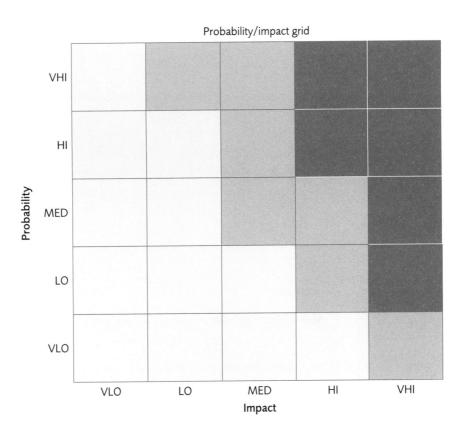

Figure 3.21 Probability impact grid

Plan responses

Having arrived at an idea of how significant a risk is, it is now necessary to determine a potential response to the risk. There are two things to do here. First, to work out what can be done to reduce the probability of the risk occurring and second, to arrange a plan and set aside contingencies to deal with it if it does happen. Some examples appear in the following table:

Table 3.2 Risk events and consequences

Risk event	Consequence	Mitigation action to reduce probability	Contingency actions to deal with it if it still does occur
Bad weather.	There may be delays in replacing the roof, thereby causing delays and potential overspend.	Do roofing work during the drier months.	Erect protective sheeting above roof while work takes place. Stop work and move workers inside during bad weather.
The new server does not arrive in time.	The software testing cannot take place.	Make sure it is purchased from a reputable supplier.	Provide a delay between planned delivery and the start of testing. Purchase two – one as a spare.
The staff do not accept the new working practices.	Poor customer service and morale.	Make sure staff are communicated with early in the process.	Have a long transition phase. Hire temporary staff while changes and alterations are made.

Generally speaking, there are eight potential responses to risks (four for threats and four for opportunities):

Threats:

- **Accept** – Here we accept the risk and take no pro-active action other than to put monitoring processes in place to make sure that the potential for damage does not change.

- **Avoid** – The only real way to avoid a risk is to change the project scope or approach – what we do or the way we do it. Remove a particular chemical from the process, for example.

- **Transfer** – We seek to move the risk from our risk log onto someone else's risk log. We seek to transfer the potential for harm to another, usually through an insurance policy or a contract.

- **Reduce** – Either the probability or the impact (or both). For example, provide training to staff so they know how to operate a process (reduces probability) or perhaps test all output so that if a poor quality product is produced, we do not deliver it to the client (reduces the impact of the risk).

Opportunities:

- **Reject** – Choose not to take advantage of the opportunity, possibly because it is worth too little or requires too much work to capitalise upon.

- **Enhance** – Take pro-active steps to make sure that, not only is the risk made more likely to happen, but also that the consequences are made more valuable. If there is a chance of finishing the hotel refurbishment early, we can seek to sell the rooms earlier.

- **Exploit** – Take no steps to enhance probability or impact and merely allow it to mature. We then take advantage of the consequences. This could perhaps be where their value is fair, but where it is not worth exposing ourselves to the increased risk involved in enhancing them.

- **Share** – Seek partners with whom we can actively capitalise on the circumstances. Often, this might take the form of a joint venture – for example, where an opportunity exists for an extra retail outlet in the bus station. As it is not core business, we may seek a partner to help capitalise on it.

Care is needed when arriving at any response to risk because, whatever action we take, there is the potential to generate other risks. For example, when changing the type of chemical used in a particular cleaning process with another to avoid risks of damaging a polished surface, we may introduce the secondary risk that the replacement chemical is not as efficient as the original, meaning that the surface remains dirty. This is an example of a secondary risk.

Implement responses

Once the specific responses have been decided upon, they should be included within the project plan. A project does not have a risk plan and a separate project plan. It simply has a new version of the plan. Therefore, once the responses have been scoped and planned, they are included within the work breakdown structures, schedules, budgets, and so on.

The project manager needs to make sure that the process is alive and continually reviewed. Risk reviews should take place at prescribed intervals, proper records kept, and escalation and advice sought where necessary. They must also make sure the team is engaged and that all available information is utilised where practical to improve the quality of the evaluations.

Use of a risk register

Once a risk has been identified, it must be recorded on a risk register and annotated with some basic information, such as:

- **Identification number** – usually sequential within a given project or programme.

- **Description** – a long-hand description, which should include the cause and effect.

- **Category** – this aids communication and might include: strategic (risks that would interfere with the organisation's interests); project (those that might cause the project to fail); operational (risks that would interfere with the organisation's business); and technical (potential problems with the products and their manufacture).

- **Potential impact** on the project objectives pre-mitigation (only possible after the assessment step – see below).

- **Probability pre-mitigation** (only possible after the assessment step – see below).

- **Potential actions** to mitigate the risk (only possible after the plan response step – see below).

- **Assignment of an owner** – a risk owner is the person or individual who is best placed to manage the risk.

The value of doing this is that the register can then be used pro-actively to manage risks going forward – it is not simply an administrative exercise to show that the process has been followed. Typically, there may also be an indication of the effect of the actions and a post-mitigation score so that the effect of committing resources is visible. The project manager typically holds this register and will need to make sure it is up to date.

Quick quiz (answers on page 158)

	Question	Options	Your answer
1	The measures against which a risk is assessed are...	a) Power and influence b) People and information c) Probability and influence d) Probability and impact	
2	Which of these is not a stage in the APM risk management process?	a) Initiater b) Plan response c) Quantitative d) Assess	
3	Brainstorming involves _____ people?	a) Two b) One c) Three d) As many as needed	

	Question	Options	Your answer
4	Throughout the project, risk scores will change...	a) Once b) Never c) Potentially many times d) At the end	
5	Which of these is not a risk identification technique?	a) Brainstorming b) Expert judgement c) Guesswork d) Assumptions analysis	

BIKEWEB CASE STUDY

"I know lots of things could go wrong – the question is, what shall we do about it?"

"We could get hit by a meteorite."

"Yes, Lottie, we could get hit by a meteorite. If that happens, then this project will probably be the least of our worries."

"Or an asteroid."

"Yes...or an asteroid. Can we all just try and think of sensible things that might go wrong with the plan so we can start to think of things to try and stop them going wrong?"

Jayne gave out some sticky notes again. They all started scribbling things down and Jayne asked them to put them up onto the probability impact grid she had drawn on the flipchart.

"Right then, so it looks like the most likely thing to go wrong is that the web designers don't get their bits done on time." Everyone nodded. "Very high impact – high probability." "Why is it high?" She was genuinely concerned – she thought they were working quite well together already.

" 'Cos they're useless?" Sue suggested.

"Really? I thought they were getting on OK."

"Have you seen the colour scheme they've come up with? Purple!"

FUNDAMENTALS

"OK, but apart from that, do we have genuine concerns?" They all nodded and mumbled some words like 'awkward', 'late' and 'not communicative'.

Jayne made a note to get hold of the account manager and get an update as soon as she had finished writing up the risk log. This was valuable information that was really useful in determining what risks there were and how important they might be.

To be continued...

Learning exercise

What other risks do you think appear on Jayne's risk log? How significant are they? For one that you identify, see if you can come up with a plan to try to prevent it happening. Draw them on a probability/impact grid like the one below:

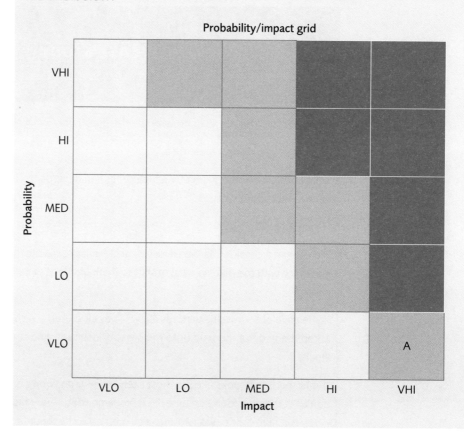

Probability/impact grid

Use this space to make some notes

....

....

....

....

....

....

3.7 | Quality management

By completing this sub-section you will be able to:

- define quality;
- define quality management;
- define quality planning, quality assurance, quality control, continual improvement.

Quality and quality management

Definition – quality

'The fitness for purpose or the degree of conformance of the outputs of a process or the process itself.'

APM Body of Knowledge 6th edition

Definition – quality management

'Quality management is a discipline for ensuring that outputs, benefits, and the processes by which they are delivered, meet stakeholder requirements and are fit for purpose.'

APM Body of Knowledge 6th edition

Please note that these definitions apply not only to the products of the project but also, importantly, to the extent to which the project conforms to its own processes (i.e. was the plan instrumental in delivering the quality outputs). There is great deal of significance to the term quality and it is worth spending time looking at it in more detail.

If I want to travel cheaply and easily by car, a small hatchback may be just what is required. In this respect the car conforms to my requirements and specification and is therefore deemed to be a 'quality' product. If I wish to transport a family of six in comfort, I may need some form of large MPV. This then would be a quality car and the hatchback would not be. Quality is a binary decision. The product either fulfils the requirements and specification, or it does not.

Often the term 'quality' is applied to the assessment of a product without really knowing what was expected. In these cases, the perspective will be totally subjective and open to interpretation. Inevitably, there are occasions when a subjective analysis carries a lot more weight than the purely objective analysis against a pre-agreed specification – for example, with a stay in a hotel, the customer experience is more than just the size of the room.

The nature of the product is specified as part of the work package descriptions and will carry associated acceptance criteria. It is the achievement of these acceptance criteria that formally acknowledges that the requirements have been met.

Quality pervades everything we do and what we produce. It is an integral component of professional project management directed full square at producing the right product first time, every time. Importantly, quality includes not only the fitness for purpose of project products (deliverables) but also the extent to which the project conforms to its own processes (i.e. was the plan instrumental in delivering the quality outputs).

Quality management

There are four components in quality management:

1. Quality planning – is the process of determining which quality standards are necessary and how to apply them. The project must produce a quality management plan (part of the PMP) and in it describe how the project will produce quality products and how it will be managed, including what processes and measurements will be used. It will describe all of the following:

- the roles and responsibilities concerned with quality – these might include quality assurance testing, supervision and management roles;

- the processes that will be followed – these will be documented in a systematic way and will govern the mechanisms for the production of the product specifications and testing procedures;

- how continual improvement will be actioned – this will include making adjustments to processes where they are proven to be unsatisfactory;

- what project assurance techniques will be deployed, such as audit, supplier vetting, specification writing, etc;

- what quality control techniques will be used, such as walkthroughs, flowcharts, inspection tests and measurement, etc;

- interactions with other processes (e.g. configuration management) and how these links will be established and managed.

2. Quality assurance – provides confidence to the host organisation that its projects, programmes and portfolios are being well managed. It validates the consistent use of procedures and standards, and ensures that staff have the correct knowledge, skills and attitudes to fulfil their project roles and responsibilities in a competent manner.

Assurance usually incorporates components of:

- **Training** – is the team properly trained? Are training records in place? Are there clear job requirements and are we able to vouch for the fact that the post holder is competent?

- **Audit** – can be used to make sure in a formal and external way whether or not the processes and principles of the PMP are being followed. Commissioned by sponsors, steering groups and others, they will provide evidence of the fact that things are being executed in the way intended.

- **Lessons learned** – the assurance processes make sure that the lessons learned during the project are properly communicated and that a properly formulated feedback loop is in place, making sure that mistakes and poor quality are removed at the root of the problem; the illnesses cured, not the symptoms.

Quality assurance must be independent of the project to which it applies, so it is normally conducted by the project office or quality department.

3. Quality control – includes a variety of techniques that are generally influenced by the nature of the project. For example, you would not rely on a visual inspection of safety-critical software code, whereas for a small brick wall it may well be appropriate. The testing methods are therefore driven by the nature of the product.

There are a number of these techniques, some of which are discussed below. In all cases, quality control must be undertaken using an objective mechanism, comparing the finished product against a specification to confirm acceptability. Work packages will all have associated acceptance criteria.

- **Inspection and measurement** – as discussed above, very often a simple sight-check will be sufficient, looking through a document before it is sent out or looking at the way a playing surface has been laid may be all that is required, perhaps measuring the height using some form of gauge or a tape to make sure the white lines are the right distance apart. In software, the use of various levels of specification can provide the means to develop ever more precise tests to turn what might be fairly subjective requirements into testable products and systems.

- **Walkthroughs** – these are a little more in-depth and will usually involve a group of people stepping through the lines of code in a software programme, or perhaps literally walking through a finished arrivals hall to make sure the signs are in place.

4. Continual improvement – is a fundamental principle of quality. It requires the correct use of feedback and using the lessons of the past to drive the actions of the future. Projects can evolve their processes to tune and develop their approach, improving accuracy and conformance to requirements.

The benefits of a quality management process are that:

- eventually, if followed to its ultimate conclusion, it will eradicate all problems and a perfect product will be produced. This will probably never happen in reality, but as we progress towards it, faults will occur less often;

- it engenders confidence on the part of the stakeholders that they will receive what they asked for, because requirements are visibly and systematically recorded and processed. Stakeholders can therefore be more comfortable that their needs will be addressed;

- it reduces rework, thus ultimately reducing costs. This is because there will be clear specifications and direction to the effort, with clear statements of anticipated results that can be assured and checked;

- in safety-critical systems, it provides confidence that those processes will not introduce risk through faulty deliverables. Testing will be thorough and rigorous and any deviations from the specification will be spotted and dealt with at an early stage and completely;

- with a strong ethos of continual improvement, quality will improve efficiency and effectiveness over time, as lessons will be learnt and used to provide diagnostic information and guidance for the establishment of better processes going forward.

 Quick quiz (answers on page 159)

	Question	Options	Your answer
1	Quality is best described as what?	a) Fitness for purpose b) Gold plated c) Posh d) The best we can do	
2	Which of these is not a component of a quality management process?	a) Continual improvement b) Planning c) Control d) Finishing	
3	Acceptance criteria are associated with work package deliverables.	True or false?	

	Question	Options	Your answer
4	Changes to specifications need to be controlled by which other process?	a) Requirements management b) Planning c) Change control d) Project management plan	
5	Which of these is NOT a component of quality assurance?	a) Training b) Lessons learned c) Audit d) Resource management	

BIKEWEB CASE STUDY

Jayne was chatting with Sue about the problems with the web designers' work. "So, OK, they don't really ask you what you want beforehand, just give you options, and you don't like any of them?"

"Yes, sort of."

"But does the system actually work?"

"Well, yes, it does – actually, it's quite good. It's quite slick, and I don't have to keep updating all those lists of members all the time – it does it automatically."

"So, it sounds like a qualitative issue, really. Perhaps we didn't specify clearly enough what colours we wanted and how they would be used."

"I don't understand what qualitative means – I'm sorry, I'm probably being really thick."

"No – sorry. Qualitative means that the measurement is subjective, personal, like you ask for blue, they give you blue but you don't like that kind of blue. The other type is quantitative and that is where there is a specific measure that is unambiguous."

"OK, well, perhaps, but it's still a pain, as there is an awful delay getting hold of them because they're in India, and, really, bright purple! Any idiot would realise that's too brash for something like this – we need greens and browns – something more natural."

"OK, well let's convene a conference call and run through the specification to make sure we are clear about what we want. That way, we can go back to them when we need to ask them to correct things and it won't just be on matters of opinion."

FUNDAMENTALS

"It's not just my opinion, you know."

"Yes. I do – but let's write it so it's clearer. We will be on more solid ground that way."

Jayne made a note to tighten up the web specification and make sure the testing was thorough enough to pick up any other problems.

To be continued...

Learning exercise

What would you say was Jayne's most pressing problem with regard to quality? What does she have to get absolutely right?

Use this space to make some notes

4

Development

4.1   Issue management

By completing this sub-section you will be able to:

- define an issue;
- define issue management;
- explain the difference between issues and risks;
- describe the use of an issue log.

Issues

> **Definition – issue**
>
> 'A formal issue occurs when the tolerances of delegated work are predicted to be exceeded or have been exceeded. This triggers the escalation of the issue from one level of management to the next in order to seek a solution.'
>
> *APM Body of Knowledge 6th edition*

The definition needs a bit of clarification in that the word tolerance may be unclear. When a project is first commissioned and agreed, the project manager has a clear description of what they are required to do in terms of time, cost and quality written clearly and unambiguously in the PMP. The world would be very strange if the future was completely predictable and so it is reasonable to expect that the journey the project will take may vary from the plan. If these changes are significant, there is a need for change control to help understand and reflect them in a revised PMP, and the project manager would need to seek approval for these changes. However, the project manager may have agreed with the sponsor some areas where they (the project manager) have some latitude to spend a little more (or less); take a little longer (or less time) or vary the deliverables in the face of legitimate circumstances. This is called tolerance. It enables the project manager to make operational project decisions to keep things on track and to avoid seeking approval for each and every (possibly trivial) change.

Issue management is one of the key roles of a project manager. During the normal running of a project, issues should not arise. Things will have been properly planned, and no extraneous influences should interfere in such a way as to jeopardise that progress. The project manager will need to be on their guard, though, as seemingly innocuous incidents can become a major problem and, if not handled in the right way, have every opportunity to derail the project.

In short, if something happens that the project manager cannot deal with, they need to ask for help from someone else. This is called issue escalation.

It is necessary to have a process to guide this escalation, as it would not be wise simply to leave it to the project manager's memory to ensure that everything is dealt with. Also, the organisation will want to see that issues are being dealt with properly to safeguard their investment. To do this, a project manager will create an issue management plan, and this will (once again) be documented in the project management plan.

Issue management

A typical issue management process (part of the plan) will follow a number of discrete stages – for example:

Recording – the project manager will recognise the source of the issue and make arrangements to record it in a formal manner on their issue log (see below). The issue log will be where they keep the details relating to all the issues currently presenting themselves to the project. There may be some that do not require escalation, but those that do will probably be the more significant and in need of senior management intervention.

Assessing – a brief (or sometimes not so brief) period of assessment needs to take place whereby, in consultation with others, the project manager seeks to understand the nature of the issue and what potential it has for impact. For example, if the contractor has gone bust, we may not get delivery on time, so we need to do something now to fix that problem.

Planning – every issue will need a plan of action describing what needs to be done, and the project manager will need to seek approval for those plans from the senior leadership team of the project. Doing anything invariably costs money.

Escalation (if needed) – for the more serious occurrences, the project manager may need to seek assistance from elsewhere to deal with the issue. This may be from the sponsor or perhaps the steering group.

Resolution – hopefully the plans will be approved and the activity fixes the problem. During this process, the project manager may need to consider any further issues or perhaps risks that may have been generated.

Update the log – once completely fixed, the project manager will update the issue log and ensure that whoever raised the issue is informed that it has been resolved.

The issue log

Recognition of an issue should be swiftly followed by the recording of it on some form of register. This is generally referred to as the issue log maintained by the project manager (potentially supported by the project office). An example of such a template (the issue log) appears in Figure 4.1.

Issue log							
			Impact				
ID	Description	Date	Time	Cost	Owner	Category	Agreed actions

Figure 4.1 Issue log

The headings are very similar to those on a risk register and there are a lot of synergies. One significant source of issues is simply risks that have occurred. Issues can appear under other circumstances, but it can be argued that this is simply a failing on the part of the risk management process in that it has not predicted them!

The difference between issues and risks

Put simply, issues have happened and demand attention to fix the problems they have caused. Risks, on the other hand, are yet to happen (i.e. they remain in the future). If you think about it hard enough, you will conclude that a perfect risk management process enacted thoroughly will pre-empt any issue. We have thought about what could go wrong and stopped it happening. The trouble with this approach is that not every risk is foreseeable. You cannot avoid all risk. Sometimes these things will just happen, and you need a decent process to deal with them when they do.

FUNDAMENTALS

 Quick quiz (answers on pages 159–60)

	Question	Options	Your answer
1	Escalation of an issue will occur when...	a) The sponsor requests an update on the project status b) A risk register needs to be updated as a result of a project review c) The project manager is unable to deal with an issue d) A change in scope is proposed to the sponsor	
2	Which of these is NOT an issue?	a) The main provider has gone out of business part way through the project b) The cost of raw materials may go up during the development phase of the project c) The cost of raw materials has gone up and the cost will exceed the budget d) There is bad weather on the day of the opening ceremony for the project	
3	Which of these is NOT a heading on the issue log?	a) Date b) Number c) Owner d) Probability	
4	Which of these is MOST likely to cause a project to fail?	a) Not dealing with issues in a timely fashion b) Not writing and maintaining the issue log c) Mistaking issues for risks during the planning of the project d) Using the wrong format of issue log	
5	The project manager would normally write the issue management process in the ——	a) Business case b) Risk management plan c) Project management plan d) Change log	

BIKEWEB CASE STUDY

The maps are being digitised, the hosting service is live and the web design company has been appointed and is working away, producing prototypes for review, etc. Jayne is on top of things and her plan, created eight weeks ago, is still relatively unchanged and seems to be working as the baseline for the project. Things go wrong occasionally and mostly they are sorted (like having to recover from a media failure on the mapping server).

The phone rings. "Jayne Watson – BikeWeb, how can I help?"

The call is from the supplier of the piece of equipment needed for the payment gateway service, telling her that, due to production problems, the machine will be delayed by four weeks. Jayne goes into Karim's little den and taps him on the shoulder.

"Sysmech have just been on the phone. They've had a production problem, and the new gateway server will be four weeks late.

"What shall we do?"

"We talked about it, don't you remember?" He pulled out his copy of the risk log.

"You told me to make arrangements with a rental company to hire one in case the one we ordered was delayed. A risk mitigation action, you called it, as I remember. And when a risk occurs...ta-da!...an issue appears – just like now, I guess."

"And you did that."

"Yes, I did that and they are just a call away," he replied. "Shall I hustle that along?" He waved his mobile phone in the air.

"Good plan." She updated the issue log and quietly kicked herself for forgetting what they had agreed. She hated Karim when he got all smug.

All this project management stuff seemed to be working, though, so things weren't all bad.

To be continued...

Learning exercise

Try completing Jayne's entry into the issue log using these headings:

Issue number	Description	Date	Impact on time (L,M,H)	Impact on cost (L,M,H)	Owner	Action

---

Use this space to make some notes

| 4.2 | **Change control and configuration management** |

By completing this sub-section you will be able to:

- define configuration management and change control in relation to scope management;
- explain the relationship between change control process and configuration management;
- list the steps involved in a typical change control process;
- list the activities in a typical configuration management process.

Definition – configuration management

'Configuration management encompasses the administrative activities concerned with the creation, maintenance, controlled change and quality control of the scope of work.'

APM Body of Knowledge 6th edition

Definition – change control

'Change control is the process through which all requests to change the baseline scope of a project, programme or portfolio are captured, evaluated and then approved, rejected or deferred.'

APM Body of Knowledge 6th edition

Change control and configuration management processes

Configuration management

Configuration management is a process that is used to help make sure everything produced by the project (the products) are correct and conform to their own respective specifications, and in so doing ensure that mistakes and misunderstandings are minimised. These specifications are held in a place called the configuration library. A good many organisations have document management systems and in most respects these document management systems could be classified as configuration management systems.

These types of system and this rigour helps, because all the products are recorded in the same library and access to them is managed by a specialist 'librarian' who has the job of checking these products out to those who need them and checking them back into the library when they have first been produced or latterly modified. The person undertaking this role is called the configuration librarian.

To help manage all of this the configuration librarian will maintain a document called a status account, and the exact process to be followed will be written down in the project management plan in a section called 'configuration management process (or procedure)'.

As products are produced, their specifications are written and approved. These specifications are stored in the library, and thereafter they are used as a reference when the products are tested and potentially when they are changed. The changes will be undertaken as a consequence of the change control process described below, and usually the documents held in the library are recorded with version numbers that increment with each new version. It is common to see a document referred to as version 1, version 2, etc. These updates are recorded in the status account.

On a smaller project, configuration management may not be appropriate in a formal sense. The project manager will be able to keep track of the products directly and retain that information in some smaller file system that they can rely on as being current.

If a more comprehensive configuration management process is required, there are a number of accepted steps that can be adopted that in conjunction represent a configuration management procedure.

- **Configuration planning** – the project manager will need to make sure that an appropriate configuration management plan exists that describes how the change and configuration management processes will operate. This will form part of the PMP and contain the key roles, processes, documents and control mechanisms that will operate. For example, it will describe what the project change control will look like and what computer system may be used to store documents.

- **Configuration identification** – each product stored on the system will require an identifier. This may just be a name or a number that uniquely identifies that document. These numbers will be allocated early in the project, usually with reference to the product breakdown structure.

- **Configuration control** – the actual process of storing the documents and of checking them out and then back into the library. Carrying out the checks that the products are the right ones and which others may be affected by a given change.

- **Configurations status accounting** – the act of updating the status account to keep all the records straight. Some of the things held on the status account that are attributes of a product include the product identifier, the owner of the product, the latest version and the date it was produced.

- **Configuration verification and audit** – the whole process will need to be audited to make sure that everything is on track and as it should be. This can be a physical audit that checks that an item meets its specification, a functional audit that checks that an item meets the need or a system audit that checks that the configuration management system is being followed.

What are changes and why do they need controlling?

A change is something that will affect any of the baselines associated with a project – the time, cost, quality, risk exposure or benefits case. Some changes may be welcome – some not. Either way, they need to be managed.

Change comes about for a number of reasons:

- external influences – for example, a change of government or organisational strategies;

- a new and innovative technique or process apparent after the business case has been agreed;

- efficiencies of process and changes associated with getting things done quicker/ cheaper;

- changes to the benefits model – perhaps doing a little more may have a huge return;

- evolving designs and emergence of new information;

- contractual changes generated by the client or other stakeholders.

As time progresses, the ability to have an impact on the shape and direction of a project diminishes. Similarly, as time goes by, the cost of any changes will rise. We have examined these issues earlier in this guide.

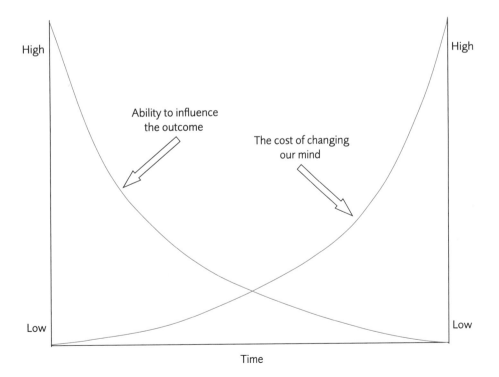

Figure 4.2 The cost of change curve

Much of the role of the project manager is devoted to the construction of plans of one form or another. Having gone to so much trouble to make sure that the plans are coherent, viable and communicated, it would be very counter-productive to allow uncontrolled change to undermine all the good work. One of the major causes of problems with projects is uncontrolled change, because ultimately it ends up with no one knowing what is going on. This uncontrolled change is called scope creep. The purpose of a change control process is to make sure that the baselines of the project are secured and only changed with appropriate controls, checks, agreement and communication.

The project manager may need to consider a simple process to instil in all the stakeholders so that scope creep does not happen. Care needs to be taken so as not to appear unhelpful and overly bureaucratic. The emphasis is on control and the ability of the project manager to keep track of and make sure that proper authorisation has been received for changes to any of the key criteria.

Interaction between configuration management and change control

If you look at change control as the maintenance of control over the scope of the project, and configuration management as the maintenance of control over the physical, technical deliverables, you will be about right. The change control process includes managerial steps to accept or reject changes to what is being done or what is being delivered. It does not in itself seek to control the progression of one state of a product to another; this is reserved for configuration management.

Key interactions between the two processes are:

- when a change control is raised, the configuration library will need to be checked to ensure that all relevant products are included in the assessment;

- when a change to a product is approved, the configuration librarian will oversee the migration of one product release to another;

- when multiple changes are needed, the configuration library will be the source to help understand which products have an impact on others;

- the configuration library will hold the details of the individual configuration item owners – those who need to be consulted about changes.

An example change control process

Figure 4.3 describes the minimum steps that should be included within a change control process to be sure to control a project's scope.

Change request

A change can emanate from a number of sources and for any of the reasons described above. Stakeholders may instigate a change and the project manager must make sure that change requests are recorded and expedited accordingly. Changes have the potential to

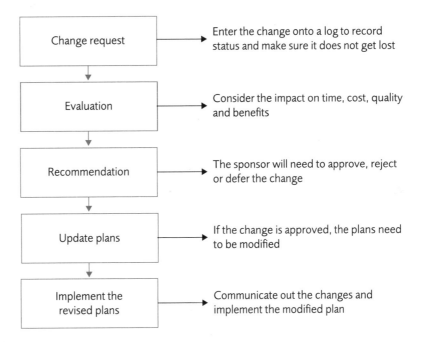

Figure 4.3 Steps in a simple change control process

impact one or all of the project's time, cost or quality success criteria. A simple change register should include a minimum of fields to properly record change requests. Generally fields to consider are:

■ number – some form of identifier to uniquely identify the request;

■ originator – who requested the change?

■ description – a brief overview;

■ date – date it was raised;

■ status – has it been accepted, rejected, deferred or approved?

■ impact – what will the effect be on the time, cost, quality, benefits and risk parameters for the project?

Evaluation

The main use of the change control register is to keep track of the various changes that will be recorded on the change control forms. These will generally be more detailed and will usually have a significant amount of other reference documents associated with them. A change control form will carry detailed analysis of the material in the change control register. It is, in essence, a 'mini business case' for the change. Similar things need to be considered with any change as with the original business case, including the impact on costs, timescales, benefits and risks. The sponsor will need to have enough information on the impact of the change to make rational decisions about whether to approve them or not.

During the assessment, all the product specifications from the configuration libraries are analysed and the impacts of changes to the products are evaluated to make sure that any impacts are properly understood and any subsidiary change requests are raised.

Recommendation

The person with the authority to approve a change is the project sponsor. They have the responsibility to make sure that the stakeholders are consulted and any differences are resolved. They will liaise with the project manager and any other advisors to make sure that they are in essence 'doing the right thing'. The options for the sponsor are:

1. Accept the change and authorise its inclusion into the plans.

2. Reject the change and not approve its implementation.

3. Defer the change until later.

At all stages, the stakeholders need to be communicated with and kept up to date with progress and decisions. Ultimately, the project manager will need to co-ordinate the implementation of the change to make sure that it is done seamlessly and incorporated into the plans. Once approved, a change control will have the effect of moving one or all of the project's baselines.

Update plans

This stage involves the project manager introducing the new tasks into the plan. Most of the normal planning process would already have been carried out during the detailed feasibility, but now the live schedules, budgets, specifications and risk registers will need to be formally updated and managed through the configuration management procedures. Changes must be considered alongside the existing frameworks of product descriptions and specifications. Once again the configuration librarian will be involved to make sure that the appropriate version number, modification levels and releases are coordinated.

Everyone who needs to know must be told about the change, or else errors due to incorrect information may creep into the system. It should not be forgotten that a prospective change is substantially easier to implement than retrospective changes to products already completed.

Implementation

The implementation of a change is concerned with actually carrying out the approved work. At this point, the change control process merges with the normal activities of the routine management of the plan. The project manager should maintain any changes within the main project. Once approved, the changes will be absorbed into every level of planning, and the new activities will be undertaken in exactly the same way as the original task load.

Quick quiz (answers on pages 160–61)

	Question	Options	Your answer
1	A configuration is best described as…	a) The set of functional and physical characteristics of a final deliverable defined in the specification b) The complete set of the project work packages as defined in the project scope c) The setting and options that are established to control the way in which a system operates d) Created by combining the work breakdown structure with the organisational breakdown structure	
2	A configuration management system is…	a) Independent from the change control system b) Tightly integrated with the planning process c) Very closely aligned with change control d) Not relevant to change control	
3	The steps in a change control process include request_____, assessment _____, implementation	a) Review; decision b) Changes; configuration c) Initial investigation; update plans d) Update; appraisal	
4	Who has authority to approve changes?	a) The sponsor b) The project manager c) The users d) The team	
5	Which of these is not an outcome from the assessment stage?	a) Deferral b) Rejection c) Absorption d) Approval	

BIKEWEB CASE STUDY

"Zak, I know you own the firm, but you cannot come along at this late stage and declare that you want us to roll out a mobile app, too. I know we are good at IT, but we are up to our necks and we are trying to get this website finished to plan so we can launch it at the show. Colin – tell him."

Zak didn't even give him time to speak. "I've just seen that the profit from one of the apps launched by another company I own is making three times more money than the website version. We have to get with the times and keep up with modern technology. The app was always part of this project as far as I was concerned. I specifically remember telling you about it when we first met. You can't have been listening to what I said."

Jayne looked blankly at him and said: "I know you said the app was coming along later, but it was not in the business case or the project management plan. Anyway, the website will work fine on a mobile phone if we design it to the specification, and we won't have to pay royalties to the phone manufacturer to get in their store."

"Don't get all technical on me – you know I didn't go through those documents with a fine-tooth comb. It's my company, and if I want to include the app in the project, that is what we are going to do," said Zak, trying to stay calm.

"OK then, I will look at the impact on the web project, and then raise a change control form to make sure I can let you know what the implications are before we take on the app development." Jayne said, suddenly remembering her training with Adrian.

"Well, you'd better get it done quickly, because things change fast in this technological world."

Colin stepped in and said: "Jayne, I'm sure we can resolve this. Zak, give us a bit of time – we can find a way around it."

"OK, but we won't be late...will we?"

To be continued...

Learning exercise

What do you think Jayne would write on her change control form? Try and complete this form based on the conversation with Zak:

Change control number

Description of change

Impact of change

Actions to deal with the proposed change

Owner of those actions

Change raised by

Change to be approved by

Use this space to make some notes

....

....

....

....

....

....

4.3 | Leadership and teams

By completing this sub-section you will be able to:

- define leadership;
- outline how a project team leader can influence team performance;
- define what is meant by a project team;
- outline the advantages and disadvantages of team models such as Belbin and Margerison-McCann.

FUNDAMENTALS

Leadership

Definition – leadership

'Leadership is the ability to establish vision and direction, to influence and align others towards a common purpose, and to empower and inspire people to achieve success.'

APM Body of Knowledge 6th edition

So much has been written and discussed on the nature and role of leadership, not just in the commercial world, but also in that of politics or religion. There are a huge number of varying views and opinions, and it would be impossible to try to encapsulate them all here.

The key question to be answered would have to be what team leaders do to motivate their teams. Please note the assumption here is that 'project manager' is synonymous with 'team leader'.

Project managers (leaders) may need to adjust their style of leadership according to the nature of the followers they are leading. If a follower is relatively junior and new to the role, the leader will lead by different mechanisms from those they would use to lead well established, seasoned professionals. Think of areas where you have witnessed this.

What leaders can do to influence team performance

- Help maintain and promote the project's vision both among the project team and elsewhere.

- Have energy, drive and commitment, leading by doing and motivating the team throughout project difficulties.

- Reinforce positive relationships – for example, providing clear feedback on performance.

- Build a productive project and working environment in which a focus is maintained on getting work done and moving the project forward.

- Work to raise morale by setting clear, achievable goals.

- Empower and inspire the individuals by delegating responsibility.

- Help ensure that exceptional events are resolved, and spotting opportunities as well as threats helps provide motivation.

- Ensure that productive and constructive feedback is provided to enable individual and organisational improvement.

- Protect the project from unwarranted external criticism.

Leaders will also be called upon to motivate their teams. Motivation is a vital element in the project world. It is necessary for a project manager to ensure that the staff who report to them are fully motivated, so that the problems associated with lack of motivation can be avoided. Lack of motivation will invariably result in any or all of the following unhelpful consequences:

- absence and sickness;

- poor quality of products delivered;

- interpersonal conflict;

- high staff attrition rates;

- difficulty in recruiting.

Definition – teamwork

'Teamwork is when people work collaboratively towards a common goal, as distinct from other ways that individuals can work within a group.'

APM Body of Knowledge 6th edition

This is vital in any project. At a very early stage in their career, a project manager has to come to terms with the fact that they cannot do everything themselves. They therefore need to be able to motivate others to want to do the work required. Individuals will rarely have the ability to do all of the diverse tasks on a project and therefore we need help. This, in turn, leads us down the road of having teams of multi-disciplinary individuals, all working towards a common goal – the essence of a team. The team will include all of those on the project responsible for project success.

Again, there has been a huge amount of theory developed to help understand teams and how they work. Meredith Belbin studied at Cambridge in the UK, and, with associates, developed the concept of team roles (Belbin, 2010). This has become one of the most recognisable and well-used tools to help analyse the nature of individuals and their preferred style within a team environment. One of his main conclusions was that an effective team needs to have members that between them cover nine major roles. These roles are shown in Table 4.1.

Table 4.1 Belbin's team roles descriptions

Team role		Contribution	Allowable weaknesses
Plant		Creative, imaginative, free-thinking. Generates ideas and solves difficult problems.	Ignores incidentals. Too preoccupied to communicate effectively.
Resource investigator		Outgoing, enthusiastic communicative. Explores opportunities and develops contacts.	Over-optimistic. Loses interest once initial enthusiasm has passed.
Co-ordinator		Mature, confident, identifies talent. Clarifies goals. Delegates effectively.	Can be seen as manipulative. Offloads own share of the work.
Shaper		Challenging, dynamic, thrives on pressure. Has the drive and courage to overcome obstacles.	Prone to provocation. Offends people's feelings.
Monitor/ evaluator		Sober, strategic and discerning. Sees all options and judges accurately.	Lacks drive and ability to inspire others. Can be overly critical.
Teamworker		Co-operative, perceptive and diplomatic. Listens and averts friction.	Indecisive in crunch situations. Avoids confrontation.
Implementer		Practical, reliable, efficient. Turns ideas into actions and organises work that needs to be done.	Somewhat inflexible. Slow to respond to new possibilities.
Completer/ finisher		Painstaking, conscientious, anxious. Searches out errors. Polishes and perfects.	Inclined to worry unduly. Reluctant to delegate.
Specialist		Single-minded, self-starting, dedicated. Provides knowledge and skills in rare supply.	Contributes only on a narrow front. Dwells on technicalities.

Reproduced with kind permission of Belbin (www.belbin.com)

Within the Belbin model there is no suggestion that an individual should aspire to one or another of the roles, but that they need to be exhibited somewhere within the team. Thus there is no 'perfect' profile for an individual.

What can go wrong?

If not enough attention is paid to team development, the project will not be in the best possible position. Lack of attention can lead to a number of negative circumstances that will impede progress. They are all interdependent and cannot be said to be cause-and-effect, but collectively or in isolation, they will need to be dealt with by the project management teams. Some obvious areas are:

- **Lack of motivation** – leads to high team attrition, conflict and difficulties in recruitment.

- **Poor attention to detail** – leads to rework, potential customer dissatisfaction and a lot of claims.

- **Interpersonal conflict** – leads to distress, arguments and a great deal of managerial time being consumed.

- **Lack of focus** – means idle time and increased sickness levels, time wasted on debating inconsequential issues or continual criticism.

- **Poor external perception** – means the team becomes 'not the place to work' and gains a poor reputation.

 Quick quiz (answers on page 161)

	Question	Option	Your answer
1	A leader may be able to motivate teams by...	a) Ruling with a rod of iron b) Punishing poor performance c) Adopting a different style of leadership d) Moving people to different teams	
2	Leadership is best described as...	a) A discussion between two or more parties aimed at reaching agreement b) The application of expert and specialised knowledge within a specific field and the acceptance of standards relating to that profession c) The ability to establish vision and direction, to influence and align others towards a common purpose, and to empower and inspire people to achieve success d) Accountable for ensuring that the work is governed effectively and delivers the objectives that meet identified needs	

	Question	Option	Your answer
3	Which Belbin role is suited to detailed, meticulous work?	a) Shaper b) Completer/finisher c) Plant d) Implementer	
4	Which of these is NOT a problem if there is a lack of motivation?	a) Absence b) Sickness c) Leadership d) Commitment	
5	Which of these is NOT an attribute of a leader?	a) Visionary b) Energy c) Systems-focused d) Commitment	

BIKEWEB CASE STUDY

Colin and Jayne were considering the change from Zak. "He's totally insufferable."

"Yes, I know," said Colin. "But he does own the business and inevitably has the last word."

"What shall we do, then? I really need to focus on the website."

"I know – the app development could start in parallel if we placed a contract with the developers."

"It will delay us."

"Well, what about seeing if we can get some quotes in and start a feasibility study for the app? By the time these are ready, the website will be completed."

"Yes, but even that would be more work for me and the team."

"I know, but if you got some graphics mock-ups done to show Zak, we could explain that it would be best to hold off the full development until the website is ready. I'm sure if Zak sees some progress he will be realistic."

"OK, I'd better speak to the developers."

To be continued...

<table>
<tr><td>✏️</td><td>**Use this space to make some notes**</td></tr>
</table>

....

....

....

....

....

....

4.4   Project reporting

By completing this sub-section you will be able to:

- define the purpose and benefits of project reporting.

(Project) reporting cycle

Typically, organisations will impose a tight reporting cycle for their projects to adopt. If they do not, it is still good practice for project managers to follow a standard approach each week/ month/quarter/year. A regular, formal review of progress with the team and the sponsor will be very useful, but even more so if a decent report is compiled covering off the main aspects of progress on the project. While following a fairly routine timetable, this also needs to consider the nature of the stakeholders and how to communicate with them most effectively. Methods of reporting include any of the following:

- written (such as reports);

- verbal (such as presentations);

- video;

- audio (podcasts);

- meetings;

- diagrams, charts, and tables (good for showing trends).

Here is a brief example of a typical reporting framework for reviewing and reporting progress on a project like BikeWeb.

Friday afternoon – Jayne goes around the team to see what progress had been made on each of the tasks.

Monday morning – she updates the project schedule with the new data and works out which tasks are ahead and which behind schedule.

Monday afternoon – she holds a short team meeting to discuss any issues and what needs to be done the following week, and prepares a formal update for Colin and Zak.

Tuesday morning – she sits down with Colin and Zak to obtain recognition of progress and agreement to any remedial action or changes.

This process will work for a relatively small project and should not be taken as a de facto process for all projects, as doubtless diaries and logistics will get in the way. It does, however, give a bit of an insight into how things could happen.

The purpose of reporting is so that the organisation can be satisfied that the project is being appropriately managed and that risks are being dealt with. On larger projects, during the project life cycle, there are a number of reviews (stage gate reviews, for example). During these reviews, various aspects of the project will be scrutinised to determine progress, conformance to time schedule, budget and quality targets. These reviews will require the preparation and submission of project reports. The data will be held in the project libraries and summary (or sometimes detailed) data will be gleaned and turned into information to be considered at the meeting.

At a gate review (see section 4.5), the sponsor will be looking for a demonstration that the project is progressing to plan, whereas at a stage review, the project manager will be seeking data from the project team and clarifying progress with them.

Failure to properly report progress may have some dire consequences:

■ the project is off track and remains off track; nobody is any the wiser and there is no opportunity to identify corrective actions before it is too late;

■ the risks are not identified and an otherwise well-run project slams into a problem it is not prepared for;

■ the organisation is not able to comply with its legislative or other governance obligations.

The presentation of project data will be most effective when an appropriate method is used. There will be times when a narrative will be most successful, but sometimes graphs, pictures, drawings, animations or video may be appropriate.

Quick quiz (answers on page 162)

	Question	Option	Your answer
1	A project reporting procedure will be contained in the...	a) Project risk log b) Project issue log c) Project management plan d) Project business case	
2	Regular reporting of project progress will enable...	a) Corrective actions to be taken b) Better management of risk c) Stakeholder expectation management d) All of the above	
3	Using a varied selection of media will enable...	a) Compliance with corporate rules b) Compliance with sponsor preferences c) Use of innovative technologies d) Effective communication with a range of stakeholders	
4	Reports do not necessarily need to be...	a) Timely b) Accurate c) Relevant d) Written	
5	In the early stages of a project, the collection and creation of data will help develop...	a) Lessons learned b) Change controls c) Requirements documentation d) Templates	

FUNDAMENTALS

BIKEWEB CASE STUDY

"So, these reports then...how long do they take?"

"Not long, Colin – just an hour or so each month. I just take the time records from the worksheets the team fills out and allocate the time to the work packages in the plan, add it all up and work out how much time has gone where. From that I can figure out if we are ahead or behind schedule and whether the costs are looking OK."

"And are they? OK I mean."

"Yes," Jayne replied. "Really quite good. After I have done the maths I speak to Dean, Lottie and the others to make sure they are all OK with it, and then put it into the report along with an update to the risk log and any issues. Then that's when we (you, Zak and I) sit down and have our review.

"I must say that Zak was very complimentary about it all the other day. He was very happy, as things now seem all ready to go with the show just a couple of weeks away."

"Nine days."

He laughed. "You're starting to sound like a project manager."

"And you're starting to sound like you think that that is a good thing."

To be continued...

Learning exercise

Write down the headings on Jayne's reports to Zak and Colin.

How often do you think they meet to review the report?

What other regular meetings do you think Jayne might convene?

Use this space to make some notes

| 4.5 | **Project reviews** |

By completing this sub-section you will be able to identify the purpose of:

■ gate reviews;

■ post-project reviews;

■ benefit reviews;

■ peer reviews;

■ project audits.

Project reviews

Table 4.2 Types of review

Type of review	Scope of review and outcomes
Gate reviews	Gate reviews are a formal way for the organisation to consider a project at a given stage in its development. Undertaken by the sponsor, there are usually three outcomes to a gate review – pass, pass with reservation and fail. The benefits of undertaking gate reviews are: ■ that they encourage a regular and structured control framework to ensure that progress is as it should be; ■ they encourage the development of a relationship between the project manager and their sponsor, thus developing trust; ■ they represent a documented statement of progress to demonstrate to the organisation that a requisite level of control is being undertaken.
Post-project review	These are carried out soon after the project has finished and will provide a clear forum for the production of lessons learned (see below). Similar to a stage review, they will consider how well the project did, both in terms of what it produced and the manner in which it did so. The benefits of undertaking a post-project review are that they will: ■ evaluate how the project performed and how successful it was against the delivery of its success criteria; ■ identify the way in which the project processes contributed to project success; ■ document how problems were overcome with the ability to document the causes for the purposes of lessons learned.
Benefits reviews	Only after the products have been completed and handover has been carried out can a proper evaluation of the benefits be achieved. Managed and chaired by the sponsor, these reviews will involve the thorough analysis by the business of the relevant achievement of the stated benefits as defined in the business case. The benefits of undertaking a benefits review are: ■ the project can be recognised for having 'made a difference'; ■ the organisation can review the real benefits obtained and reconcile them with the ambitions stated in the business case; ■ the review can draw out areas where benefits may not be as expected and lay plans to modify and rectify the situation.
Peer reviews	Peer reviews can be carried out more or less anytime. They are (as the name implies) intended to use colleagues of the project manager (or potentially the sponsor) to provide external scrutiny of the way in which the role is being fulfilled and the manner in which the project is being run. These are sometimes referred to as health checks (when carried out by peers of the person being reviewed). The benefits of undertaking a peer review are:

	■ it is a great way of learning through experience – both for the reviewer and the person being reviewed; ■ they have the advantage of using people who have first-hand knowledge of the task in hand and who can empathise with particular situations and provide help if needed; ■ it capitalises upon recent, up to date knowledge; ■ it is not as onerous or potentially threatening as a more rigorous audit might be.
Project audit	All through the project, the project manager and teams will have been following the approved project management plan and all the processes within it. At certain times, it will be necessary for the organisation to satisfy itself that all is as it should be on the project, and it may subject the project to an audit. This will normally be carried out by someone external to the project and will focus mainly on the adoption and observance of procedures. Audits can be undertaken for: ■ finance, where the expenditure is checked; ■ procurement to make sure there are no irregularities or breaches of process; ■ equal opportunities or HR process to make sure legislation and principles are being followed; ■ health and safety, where there will be a check to make sure all safety procedures are being properly adhered to.

 ## Quick quiz (answers on page 163)

	Question	Options	Your answer
1	Which review takes place at the end of the first two life cycle phases?	a) Gate review b) Audit c) Benefit realisation d) Risk review	
2	Which of the following reviews is external to the project?	a) Stage gate b) Audit c) Benefit realisation d) Risk review	
3	Which of these is a valid outcome of a gate review?	a) Prevent b) Pass with reservation c) Accept d) Avoid	

	Question	Options	Your answer
4	Who would normally convene a gate review?	a) The sponsor b) The project manager c) The users d) The supplier	
5	Which of these is NOT a benefit of a peer review?	a) Draw on recent experience b) Not as onerous as a more formal review c) Carried out by the sponsor d) The reviewer may also benefit	

BIKEWEB CASE STUDY

"How are the subscriptions coming on?"

"Yes – really good. The test system is working absolutely brilliantly. We had to sort out the mobile signal, but now it's just whizzing along."

"So, Sue, was it worth all the bother? The new system, I mean?" Yuri asked Sue.

"It's brilliant! It works on mobiles fine, and we've signed up about 50 today, so that's a great start. Once the other marketing kicks in, we should be home and dry."

"It will be even better when the app is launched – I don't know how Jayne managed to talk Zak around into not having it for the launch. It would have really diverted us."

Zak came over and put his hand on Jayne's shoulder.

"I can tell you I was sceptical at the start, but you've proved to me the value of this project management stuff, and now I am totally sold on the idea. In fact, I've asked my partner at Whirlwind Bikes to talk to you to see if you can help out there. I don't know what this counts as in the world of project management, Jayne, but if you want to consider it recognition of a job well done, that's good enough for me," he added,

"Post-project review," she muttered.

"I just knew you would have a name for it!" They all laughed and watched the line of people waiting to buy their BikeWeb subscriptions with quiet satisfaction.

Learning exercise

What do you think were the main gate reviews that the project had navigated through its life? At what stages was there a conscious decision to proceed?

Use this space to make some notes

Section review

1.1	Principles of project management	pages 1–20

Some examples of other things that may be success criteria for a project (other than time, cost and quality):

■ not causing any health and safety issues;

■ not upsetting residents, customers, patients (depending on the project);

■ being able to develop staff on the project.

	Business-as-usual?	Project?
A new aircraft prototype	No, although the production aircraft that follow will be	Yes
Undertaking market research for a new product launch	For the researchers this may be familiar work	Yes – we have not researched this product before
Selling tickets for a sporting event	Yes, although again this event is unique, so could equally be a project	Not for the people selling the tickets
Taking a family of four on holiday	If it's a regular spot, then maybe it's just routine	If it's a new location, then yes

What do you think Jayne was going to say to Zak? Write an agenda for her two-hour meeting with Zak and Colin.

Jayne thought the best thing to do was to go through:

a) The main reasons for the project

b) Why use project management techniques

c) The measures of success

d) The main deliverables

e) Brief discussion of roles

f) What might go wrong

g) Agreement to next steps

She thought this would be enough for now.

FUNDAMENTALS

Put these project components into the order in which they happen:

Business case

> Produced during concept this is finalised at the end of it and signed off by the sponsoring group/business.

Project management plan

> This is created during the definition phase and is finalised at the end of it, signed off by the sponsor.

End of project report

> This is produced at the end of the project to reflect lessons learned and reflect successful outcomes.

The reasons BikeWeb is running the project are to:

- replace the old, unreliable system;
- get more customers signed up – to make more money and profit;
- reduce the manual intervention involved in the current system;
- make the site easier to use;
- have an improved payment system.

	Question	Answer
1	Portfolios can include...	d) All of the above
2	Which of the following is not a project process?	c) Concept
3	How many success criteria can a project have?	d) Any number
4	Which term most fully describes deliverables?	a) Products
5	What does PMP stand for?	a) Project management plan

Is BikeWeb work a project or a programme? Why do you say that?

BikeWeb is a project. Yes, it will lead to business benefit but it is not seeking a radical change over multiple years in different disciplines or departments. It is relatively short focused and within a single organisation.

| 1.2 | The project environment | pages 21–6 |

	Question	Answer
1	Which one of these is not a PESTLE factor?	b) Risk
2	An example of a political context might be...	c) The election of a new mayor
3	A SWOT analysis considers...	d) Strengths, weaknesses, opportunities and threats
4	Which of these is not a contextual consideration?	d) Resource histogram
5	The project manager should consider the project context...	c) All the way through

What do you think was on Karim's list? See if you can come up with six environmental factors for the BikeWeb project.

	BikeWeb project
Political	The fact that Zak was quite authoritarian and liked to get his own way
Economic	Need to satisfy the bank that the benefits will be realised
Sociological	The increased use of cycles Need to make the new site appealing to a wide audience
Technological	The new technology for the website
Legal	The need to observe copyright for the maps and other content
Environmental	To use the eco-friendly routes on the maps

FUNDAMENTALS

These names (concept, definition, etc.) are not the same in different industries. Can you think of examples (from your own project experience or perhaps from observation) where you can spot one or more of the phases and what alternative names have been used? Note some examples here:

For concept you may see feasibility or option study; for definition you may see design or planning; for development you may see build or implementation; handover can be transfer to operations.

	Question	Answer
1	How many different styles of life cycle are there?	d) There is no particular restriction, many industries have their own
2	A project manager would need to understand the nature of the project and the industry it is in to make sure the life cycle is appropriate.	a) True
3	Which review happens between handover and closure and operations?	c) Post-project review
4	Who should the project manager consult when settling on the most appropriate life cycle model?	d) All of the above
5	In the project life cycle benefits are realised...	d) During operations

What would Zak's main objections be to the adoption of a formal project life cycle?

- He may well see it as slowing things down and creating bureaucracy.

- He sounds like the sort of person who is quite impatient.

- Structure might frustrate him – he may might feel like it takes away some of his flexibility.

| 1.4 | Project roles | pages 32–8 |

	Question	Answer
1	Which best describes the reporting relationship between the project sponsor and project manager?	b) The project manager reports to the sponsor for the purposes of the project
2	Who owns the business case?	b) Sponsor
3	Who owns the project management plan?	a) Project manager
4	Which of these do the users NOT do?	d) Deliver work packages
5	Changes to the project scope are ultimately approved by...	a) The sponsor

Why do you think Zak was Jayne's nominated sponsor? Do you agree with her view of who it should be?

Jayne, looks on Zak as the main funder, it is Zak's money, and although technically she works for Colin, Zak is effectively accountable for the project. It doesn't mean she cannot seek advice from Colin if she needs support from him, her line manager.

| 2.1 | The project business case | pages 41–6 |

	Question	Answer
1	When must the business case be checked for alignment to the project management plan?	d) All of the above
2	The business case is most concerned with which type of risk?	b) Risks to the completion of the project deliverables and the realisation of the project benefits
3	The business case, once written, may change...	b) By approval at any time through formal change control
4	The business case leads directly into...	a) The production of the project management plan

	Question	Answer
5	When the project is complete, who will sign off the business case as fulfilled?	c) Sponsor

2.2   Success and benefits management   pages 46–51

	Question	Answer
1	The target finish time for a project would be an example of...	a) Success criteria
2	In a typical project we might track the monthly expenditure of the project. This would be an example of...	c) Key performance indicators
3	Throughout the project the project manager needs to keep a careful track of...	d) All of the above
4	Having a sponsor who is prepared and able to make quick decisions might be an example of a...	a) Success factor
5	Reducing the expenditure on materials storage in a warehouse as a direct result of running a project is an example of what?	a) Benefit

2.3   Stakeholder management   pages 51–8

	Question	Answer
1	What are the axes on a stakeholder analysis grid?	d) Interest in the delivery of the outcome and influence over the success of the project
2	Which of these is NOT a stage in stakeholder management?	b) Promote the interests of the key stakeholders
3	A definition of a stakeholder is...	d) The organisations or people who have an interest or role in the project, programme or portfolio, or are impacted by it

	Question	Answer
4	Which of these is NOT a difficulty with assessing a stakeholder's position on the stakeholder grid?	b) Interest and influence are the axis labels
5	Understanding the culture and expectations of stakeholders on a project will be key to understanding which project manager to appoint. Which is the most appropriate approach?	b) The selection of the project manager should take into account the stakeholder culture and expectations

Draw your own version of the stakeholder grid and populate it with the BikeWeb stakeholders.

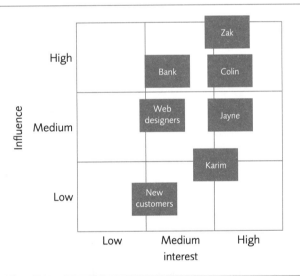

2.4 | Communications   pages 59–64

	Question	Answer
1	Who owns and manages the communication plan?	d) The project manager
2	Which of the following statements relating to the communication plan is true?	c) The communication plan is part of the project management plan
3	How do you know if communication has been successful?	c) The effectiveness of project communication can be measured by evaluating feedback from the key stakeholders
4	Which of these is NOT an example of a barrier to communication?	d) Planning

FUNDAMENTALS

	Question	Answer
5	The making of hand gestures when speaking is an example of what?	c) Body language

3.1	**The project management plan**	**pages 65–72**

	Question	Answer
1	Which statement best describes the ownership of the project management plan?	b) The project manager owns the management plan but it should be developed with the wider team
2	Which of these is NOT contained in the project management plan?	a) The investment appraisal for the project
3	Changes to the project management plan are approved by...	d) The project sponsor
4	A policy-level plan is...	c) A series of plans that set out the principles of how each aspect of the work will be managed
5	Once the PMP is agreed, it is shared with...	d) Anybody with a direct involvement with the project

Who do you think ought to be reading Jayne's project management plan? Who should have a copy?

Jayne will want to share it with all of her immediate stakeholders for their information. She may want to provide some of it to the various suppliers (like the web design company) and possibly even the bank to satisfy them that things are being run well.

3.2	**Scope management**	**pages 72–80**

	Question	Answer
1	OBS means...	c) Organisation breakdown structure
2	WBS means...	d) Work breakdown structure

	Question	Answer
3	Each level of the WBS will be easily identifiable as a sub-level of the level...	c) Above
4	Scope is defined as...	b) Including outputs, but may be extended to cover benefits
5	A RAM chart shows what?	b) The work package and the person involved in it

Write down here what you think are the main elements of the BikeWeb project scope – what is included in the project?

■ The creation of a new database of maps.

■ A new computer server.

■ Integration with the automated payments.

■ Testing of everything.

■ Conversion of the maps from the originals from the suppliers.

■ Road survey and documentation of the routes to be loaded onto the system.

FUNDAMENTALS

| 3.3 | Estimating | pages 80–4 |

BikeWeb

If you had to estimate how long it would take to load the various maps and the routes to the website, how would you do it?

- Number of maps multiplied by the time per map to convert and digitise them.

- Number of routes multiplied by the time taken to survey the routes and digitise them.

	Question	Answer
1	A ____ estimate will compare one project with another, similar project.	c) Comparative
2	Which is the best description of a comparative estimate?	a) Comparative, or analogous, estimating uses historical data from similar projects or programmes to extrapolate estimates for new work
3	What other technique is fundamental to the creation of a bottom-up estimate?	c) WBS
4	Whom should the project manager consult in the creation of estimates?	d) All of the above
5	Input to parametric estimates might NOT include what?	d) PERT

<table>
<tr><td colspan="2" style="background:#333;color:#fff;">3.4 Scheduling</td><td style="text-align:right;">pages 85–96</td></tr>
</table>

	Question	Answer
1	What is a visual representation of a project's planned activity against a calendar called?	a) A Gantt chart
2	Total float is the difference between latest finish and...	c) Early finish
3	For the precedence diagram below, what is the total duration of the project	a) 20 days
4	A milestone has what amount of time associated with it?	c) Zero
5	The critical path is the...	b) Sequence of activities through a precedence diagram from start to finish, the sum of whose durations determines the overall duration

For question 3, the precedence diagram shows activities:
- A (5)
- B (5)
- D (5)
- F (5)
- C (4)
- E (4)

What do you think the key dates are in the BikeWeb project? Where would you put Jayne's milestones? These are some examples:

- the date of the exhibition;

- the date by which all the data is loaded and testing can start;

- the date by which the web hosting company have the service ready for use.

| 3.5 | **Project resource management and procurement** | | pages 97–101 |

		Question	Answer
	1	Resource planning needs to be done when?	d) Over and over again as necessary
	2	Which of these is a type of resource?	c) Re-usable
	3	Which of these is an example of a re-usable resource?	b) People
	4	What does ITT stand for?	c) Invitation to tender
	5	Against what would a supplier's tender be judged?	d) Compliance matrix

| 3.6 | **Risk management** | pages 101–11 |

		Question	Answer
	1	The measures against which a risk is assessed are...	d) Probability and impact
	2	Which of these is not a stage in the APM risk management process?	c) Quantitative
	3	Brainstorming involves ____ people?	d) As many as needed
	4	Throughout the project, risk scores will change...	c) Potentially many times
	5	Which of these is not a risk identification technique?	c) Guesswork

What other risks do you think appear on Jayne's risk log? How significant are they? For one that you identify, see if you can come up with a plan to try to prevent it happening.

- Supplier of maps or IT goes bankrupt;

- important member of staff (Karim) goes off sick.

3.7	Quality management	pages 111–16

	Question	Answer
1	Quality is best described as what?	a) Fitness for purpose
2	Which of these is not a component of a quality management process?	d) Finishing
3	Acceptance criteria are associated with work package deliverables.	True
4	Changes to specifications need to be controlled by which other process?	c) Change control
5	Which of these is NOT a component of quality assurance?	d) Resource management

What would you say was Jayne's most pressing problem with regard to quality? What does she have to get absolutely right?

■ The bank transactions;

■ the routes have to appeal to the people who will download them to improve the company's reputation;

■ the system has to be easy to use.

4.1	Issue management	pages 117–22

	Question	Answer
1	Escalation of an issue will occur when...	c) The project manager is unable to deal with an issue
2	Which of these is NOT an issue?	b) The cost of raw materials may go up during the development phase of the project

FUNDAMENTALS

	Question	Answer
3	Which of these is NOT a heading on the issue log?	d) Probability
4	Which of these is MOST likely to cause a project to fail?	a) Not dealing with issues in a timely fashion
5	The project manager would normally write the issue management process in the ____	c) Project management plan

Try completing Jayne's entry into the issue log using these headings:

Issue number	Description	Date	Impact on time (L,M,H)	Impact on cost (L,M,H)	Owner	Action
001	The gateway server supplier has notified us of a delay in delivery	Today	H	H	Karim	Call up the loan server to use for the time being – look into recovering costs from Sysmech

4.2 Change control and configuration management pages 123–31

	Question	Answer
1	A configuration is best described as...	a) The set of functional and physical characteristics of a final deliverable defined in the specification
2	A configuration management system is...	c) Very closely aligned with change control
3	The steps in a change control process include request ____, assessment ____, implementation.	a) Review; decision

	Question	Answer
4	Who has authority to approve changes?	a) The sponsor
5	Which of these is not an outcome from the assessment stage?	c) Absorption

What do you think Jayne would write onto her change control form? Try and complete this form based on the conversation with Zak:

Change control number – 001

Description of change – The incorporation of a mobile app into the scope of the project

Impact of change – It may cause delays and over run on cost

Actions to deal with the proposed change – Need to evaluate it carefully, hold some brief meetings to consider the impact and whether it can be done

Owner or those actions – Jayne

Change raised by – Zak

Change to be approved by – Zak

4.3 Leadership and teams   pages 131–7

	Question	Answer
1	A leader may be able to motivate teams by...	c) Adopting a different style of leadership
2	Leadership is best described as...	c) The ability to establish vision and direction, to influence and align others towards a common purpose, and to empower and inspire people to achieve success
3	Which Belbin role is suited to detailed, meticulous work?	b) Completer/finisher
4	Which of these is NOT a problem if there is a lack of motivation?	c) Leadership
5	Which of these is NOT an attribute of a leader?	c) Systems-focused

FUNDAMENTALS

	4.4	**Project reporting**	**pages 137–41**

	Question	Answer
1	A project reporting procedure will be contained in the...	c) Project management plan
2	Regular reporting of project progress will enable...	d) All of the above
3	Using a varied selection of media will enable...	d) Effective communication with a range of stakeholders
4	Reports do not necessarily need to be...	d) Written
5	In the early stages of a project, the collection and creation of data will help develop...	c) Requirements documentation

Write down the headings on Jayne's reports to Zak and Colin.

How are we progressing against plan for:

a) Deliverables

b) Costs

c) Products delivered (how many).

What are the forecasts to complete everything (how much money and time)?

Are there any new risks?

Are there any new issues?

How often do you think they meet to review the report?

They would probably meet weekly (Colin and Jayne) and maybe fortnightly for Zak to be included. It is only a 14-week project, so monthly might be too infrequent – at least early on.

What other regular meetings do you think Jayne might convene?

She will need to meet with the team weekly and the suppliers similarly, but probably by telephone or video conference.

| 4.5 | **Project reviews** | **pages 141–5** |

	Question	**Answer**
1	Which review takes place at the end of the first two life cycle phases?	a) Gate review
2	Which of the following reviews is external to the project?	b) Audit
3	Which of these is a valid outcome of a gate review?	b) Pass with reservation
4	Who would normally convene a gate review?	a) The sponsor
5	Which of these is NOT a benefit of a peer review?	c) Carried out by the sponsor

What do you think were the main gate reviews that the project had navigated through its life? At what stages was there a conscious decision to proceed?

■ They would need to review the project once the business case and the funding was secured.

■ Jayne ought to have got a formal agreement to the completed plan before starting work.

Case study

BIKEWEB

BikeWeb

BikeWeb is a small company that maps cycle routes and uploads way-marked maps and GPS co-ordinates for cycle routes. In the past, conventional satellite navigation systems have been used but these are optimised for motor vehicles and have sometimes tried to direct pedal cyclists onto main roads and not to the more pleasurable (and safer) cycle paths and byways. The firm has been struggling to get its message out there, though.

The current website was originally designed and built in-house and is very 'user-unfriendly' and unreliable. This means that the billing for the various packages on sale was extremely labour-intensive and prone to failure, causing a number of customers to abort their transactions before completing them.

As part of the UK Government's drive to promote small, environmentally-friendly enterprises, BikeWeb has been awarded £10,000 from the Small Business Enterprise Scheme (SBES) to help fund a new website to promote itself, relaunch its website and invigorate its e-commerce business.

The task in hand, therefore, will involve setting the project up and making sure it is delivered in time for the company exhibition season, which starts at the round-Britain bike race in nine months' time. You know that there is a competitor company trying to develop a similar proposition as you, and they, too, are developing a new site – indeed, one of your junior staff has left to join them.

If the website is a success, the payments from direct debits and standing orders for the regular map updates will be quite large, but also if the 'on demand' service takes off, small payments of even £1 a time will all add up. The business plan shows revenues from the new service and complementary apps increasing by about £100,000 in the first year, with a further projected increase of around 30 per cent a year thereafter for about five years.

BikeWeb is owned by the original founder Zak Shallow, (who also owns a high-technology bike manufacturer in the North East and various other companies). There are eight employees, including Colin Montgomery, the general manager, Jayne Watson, the office and accounts manager, Karim Zahir, the IT manager, Charlotte Dixon, Yuri Pavlov and Dean Baker, the analysts responsible for the maps themselves, and Sue Marin, who is the membership and subscriptions manager. Yuri also helps Karim out on the IT front when necessary. Sue spends a lot of her time updating user details from lists output by the website. The maps need to be purchased from the wholesale supplier and converted and digitised to be suitable for the new system, as well as indexed to suit the way they will be made available.

So the project is key to the business; the analysts are busy digitising routes and uploading them ready to be catalogued onto the new site. They also have to go and ride the routes to make sure they are OK. The site will need to be designed, a general layout format and colour scheme devised, some new computers bought and installed, internet lines upgraded and content loaded, tested and commissioned. The electronic payment service also needs to be validated with the back end of the website – something that is known to be quite tricky to get right.

A specialist website design firm in India called E-Fit has been identified which is very experienced in the field of GPS and mapping technology, but their references have not been marvellous and some of their customers have not been altogether happy with their work. The time delay in getting bugs fixed is a real problem for them. A bit more work needs to take place with them before contracts are agreed.

To satisfy the stringent bank e-commerce tests, the company will have to demonstrate that the new site, once built, has been thoroughly tested and can reliably send on payments and receive valid acknowledgements from the bank. It must also be able to cope with serving the volume of data to multiple smart phone devices without bottlenecks and delay.

The grant is not going to be enough to pay for the new site and so a bank loan will need to be obtained for the balance.

Exam know-how

Hints and tips

Given the need to answer 60 questions in 60 minutes (one hour), you will fairly self-evidently need to try to answer one per minute.

Make sure that if you miss out a question you leave blank the relevant line on the answer sheet. It is quite distressing to come to the end of the answer sheet only to realise you still have some empty spaces on the bottom of it when you have run out of questions.

Stay focused and don't panic.

The most important point about any exam is obvious — make sure you read the question.

If you make an error on a paper-based examination answer sheet, you need to correct the mistake with the eraser provided, and on the screen the instructions will be quite clear.

Make sure you are properly prepared.

In the run-up to the exam, you might be nervous and stressed. It is easy to say, but try not to let it get in the way.

■ Avoid alcohol.

■ Get a good night's sleep.

■ Arrive early; select a decent seat near the window, out of the sun and not right under the air conditioning unit (noisy and cold).

■ Read the exam guidance from APM and make sure you have everything you need.

There are concessions for previously advised medical conditions – check the latest guidance notes.

Revision tips

Make sure you have read these sections and the associated sample multiple choice questions that go with them, to be sure you know the basics (e.g. a description of project risk management).

If you are not very good at remembering things, try writing them on an index card, turning it over and writing it again. Check if you got it right. Keep doing this and eventually it will stick.

Try to set yourself a reasonable revision plan – little and often. Set a timeframe for revising and stick to it.

Try not to just keep revising the things you already know. Try learning the things you don't know. Avoid the comfort of familiar territory. Push yourself to explore new areas that you may have considered too obscure or difficult. Some of the less popular topic areas can in fact be relatively straightforward with the right approach.

FUNDAMENTALS

If you really don't 'get' one topic, you can at a pinch leave it out of your revision schedule. Avoid leaving too many out, though, as you will probably get a question on most of the assessment criteria.

Sample exam questions

1. A communication management plan identifies the relevant information that should be communicated to:

a. The project team.

b. The project stakeholders.

c. The project board.

d. The project sponsor.

2. Which one of the following statements is <u>true</u>?

a. Independent reviews and quality audits form part of quality assurance to ensure the project manager delivers on time and to budget.

b. Quality assurance provides confidence to stakeholders that requirements for quality will be exceeded.

c. Quality control verifies that the project deliverables conform to specification, are fit for purpose and meet stakeholder expectations.

d. Quality planning enables the project manager to manage the trade-off between customer expectations and budget.

3. Project risk management is <u>best</u> described as:

a. Managing responses to threats.

b. Identifying and acknowledging threats and opportunities.

c. Planning responses to threats.

d. Minimising threats and maximising opportunities.

4. Which one of the following <u>best</u> describes a project issue?

a. A major problem that requires formal escalation.

b. A problem that the project manager has to deal with on a day-to-day basis.

c. An uncertain event that may or may not occur.

d. An opportunity that occurs through change control.

5. Scheduling can <u>best</u> be defined as the process used to determine:

a. Overall project duration.

b. Project cost estimating.

c. The project management plan.

d. Sub-contractor's responsibilities.

6. Which one of the following statements is <u>true</u>?

a. An increase in project scope is likely to increase project cost.

b. A decrease in the project time is likely to increase project quality.

c. An increase in the project quality requirements is likely to decrease project cost.

d. A decrease in the project cost is likely to decrease project time.

7. Which one of the following statements <u>best</u> defines the purpose of a product breakdown structure (PBS)?

a. To define the hierarchy of deliverables that are required to be produced on the project.

b. To define how the products are produced by identifying derivations and dependencies.

c. To establish the extent of work required prior to project commissioning and the handover.

d. To identify the health and safety strategies and procedures to be used on the project.

8. Which one of the following is <u>least</u> likely to be a success criteria?

a. A target for the project to receive zero change requests.

b. The date by which the project is to be completed.

c. Delivery of products that meet required specifications.

d. The awarding of bonuses to senior management.

9. Which one of the following is a <u>valid</u> project key performance indicator (KPI)?

a. Staff appraisals.

b. Management buy in.

c. Milestone achievement.

d. Master schedule.

10. Which one of the following statements is <u>true</u>?

a. The business case is owned by the sponsor and is created during the concept phase of the project life cycle.

b. The business case is owned by the project manager and is created during the concept phase of the project life cycle.

c. The business case is owned by the sponsor and is created during the definition phase of the project life cycle.

d. The business case is owned by the project manager and is created during the definition phase of the project life cycle.

11. Who owns the project management plan (PMP)?

a. The project team.

b. The chief executive.

c. The project manager.

d. The project support office.

FUNDAMENTALS

12. Which one of the following <u>best</u> describes users?

a. Providers of both strategic and tactical direction to the project.

b. Those intended to receive benefits or operate outputs.

c. Facilitators of an appropriate issue resolution procedure.

d. Those providing full-time commitment to the project.

13. Which statement <u>best</u> describes a responsibility of the project manager:

a. To be the sole source of expertise for estimating techniques on cost and time.

b. To deliver the project objectives to enable benefits to be realised.

c. To take ultimate accountability for the delivery of the business benefits.

d. To delegate all accountability for managing time, cost and quality to team leaders.

14. A project is <u>typically</u> defined in terms of scope, time, cost and which other parameter?

a. Benefits.

b. Quality.

c. Tolerance.

d. Controls.

15. Which one of the following statements is <u>true</u>?

a. Business-as-usual activities cannot be improved.

b. Business-as-usual activities are more difficult to manage than projects.

c. Projects are transient endeavours that bring about change to business-as-usual.

d. A project is always the starting point for operation refinement.

16. What is defined as "the ability to influence and align others towards a common purpose"?

a. Teamwork.

b. Motivation.

c. Management.

d. Leadership.

17. Which one is a <u>true</u> statement relating to project communications?

a. A project sponsor is responsible for all communication methods and media.

b. Different stakeholders typically have different communication needs.

c. It is best to have a standard set of project reports used for every project.

d. Email is the only way to communicate with large numbers of people.

18. In project management, the term quality is <u>best</u> defined as:

a. Inspection, testing and measurement.

b. Reviews and audits.

c. Fitness for purpose of deliverables.

d. Professionally-bound project reports.

19. The <u>main</u> outcome of risk identification, in a risk management process, is to:

a. Identify and determine the relative importance of the project risks.

b. Identify and describe all risks that might occur on the project.

c. Identify and determine the responses to the project risks.

d. Identify and describe risks that have occurred on previous projects.

20. Which one of the following is <u>not</u> considered in resource management?

a. Identifying resources.

b. Influencing resources.

c. Assigning resources to activities.

d. Matching resources to the schedule.

21. Which one of the following does project change control <u>primarily</u> seek to ensure?

a. All variance to the project scope is evaluated.

b. No reduction in the perceived quality of the project outcome.

c. Management costs of the project do not increase.

d. Any decrease in the scoped deliverable of the project is rejected.

22. Which one of the following is captured in the Work Breakdown Structure (WBS)?

a. The life cycle phases.

b. The logical order of tasks.

c. The scope of the project.

d. Project costs.

23. Project reporting can <u>best</u> be defined as:

a. Informing stakeholders about the project.

b. Storing and archiving of project information.

c. Gathering stakeholder feedback.

d. Collecting project information.

24. Which one of the following statements <u>best</u> defines an estimate?

a. An approximation of project time and cost targets, refined throughout the project life cycle.

b. A prediction of a future condition or event based on information or knowledge available now.

c. The value of useful work done at any given point in a project to give a measure of progress.

d. A situation that affects or influences the outcome of the project expressed in time or cost terms.

25. The justification for the investment to be made in a project is documented in the:

a. Cost breakdown structure.

b. Procurement strategy.

c. Business case.

d. Project management plan.

26. Which one of the following is a responsibility of the project steering group/board?

a. To identify potential problems for the project team to solve.

b. To provide strategic direction and guidance to the sponsor.

c. To manage the project team in all daily activities.

d. To receive and consider daily reports from team members.

27. One of the reasons a project life cycle is split into phases is to:

a. Facilitate formal go/no-go decision making during the project.

b. Balance the costs of work in each phase of project development.

c. Mirror the major deployments of resources throughout the project.

d. Chunk work into time periods of similar durations.

28. Which of the following best describes a project environment?

a. The type of organisation concerned with implementation.

b. The structured method used to control the project.

c. The context within which a project is undertaken.

d. An understanding of the risks involved in the project.

29. Which one of the following statements best describes a project?

a. A project is a set of tools and techniques often used when delivering organisational change.

b. A project is the sum of activities needed to remove uncertainty from a unique piece of work.

c. A unique transient endeavour undertaken to achieve a desired outcome.

d. A project is a method of planning work.

30. The document that identifies what information needs to be shared, to whom, why, when and how is called the:

a. Communication management plan.

b. Stakeholder mapping grid.

c. Document distribution schedule.

d. Responsibility assignment matrix.

31. An important aim of a post-project review is to:

a. Validate overall progress to date against the budget and schedule.

b. Capture learning and document it for future usage.

c. Ensure acceptance of all permanent documentation, signed by the sponsor.

d. Establish that project benefits have been identified.

32. The process that evaluates overall project performance to provide confidence is called:

a. Quality assurance.

b. Quality planning.

c. Quality control.

d. Quality audit.

33. Which one of the following statements about the project risk register is <u>false</u>?

a. It facilitates the review and monitoring of risks.

b. It facilitates the risk appetite.

c. It facilitates the recording of risk responses.

d. It facilitates the recording of risks.

34. Which one of the following statements <u>best</u> defines procurement?

a. A technique to establish the best approach for obtaining the resources for the project.

b. A group of interrelated resources and activities that transform inputs into outputs.

c. The description of the purpose, form and components to support delivery of a product.

d. The process by which products and services required for the project are acquired.

35. Once a change has been requested what is the next step in the change control process?

a. Evaluate the change.

b. Advise the sponsor.

c. Update the change log.

d. Update the project plan.

36. A responsibility assignment matrix (RAM) can be used to:

a. Define the terms of reference of the project manager.

b. Define the limits of the project sponsor's responsibilities.

c. Allocate risk management response activities to project personnel.

d. Allocate work packages to those responsible for project work.

37. An organisational breakdown structure (OBS) is used to identify:

a. The reporting structure and current availability of all individuals in the project.

b. Technical ability and line of communication for all individuals in the project.

c. Lines of communication and responsibility for all the individual managers in the project.

d. The reporting structure and lines of communication for all individuals in the projects.

FUNDAMENTALS

38. Which one of the following <u>best</u> describes project success criteria?

a. Actively seeking some senior management support.

b. Measures by which the success of the project is judged.

c. Achievement of milestones.

d. A motivated project team.

39. Comparative estimating uses:

a. Current data from similar projects.

b. Historic data from all projects.

c. Historic data from similar projects.

d. Current data from all projects.

40. Which one of the following <u>best</u> describes a project stakeholder?

a. A party who is concerned about the project going ahead.

b. A party with an interest or role in the project or is impacted by the project.

c. A party who has a vested interest in the outcome of the project.

d. A party who has a financial stake in the organisation managing the project.

41. The <u>main</u> purpose of the project management plan is to:

a. Provide justification for undertaking the project in terms of evaluating the benefit, cost and risk of alternative options.

b. Ensure the project sponsor has tight control of the project manager's activity.

c. Document the outcomes of the planning process and provide the reference document for managing the project.

d. Document the outcome of the risk, change and configuration management processes.

42. Who has ultimate responsibility for project risk?

a. Steering group.

b. Risk owner.

c. Project sponsor.

d. Project manager.

43. When a project has completed the handover and closure phase:

a. The project deliverables are ready for commissioning.

b. The project deliverables are ready for handing over to the users.

c. The project documentation must be disposed of.

d. The capability is now in place for the benefits to be realised.

44. Which one of the following illustrates why effective project management is beneficial to an organisation?

a. It utilises resources as and when required under direction of a project manager.

b. It advocates employing a consultancy firm that specialises in managing change.

c. It recommends using only highly skilled people in the project team.

d. It ensures that the chief executive is accountable for the achievement of the defined benefits.

45. A <u>key</u> aspect of managing a project involves:

a. Defining which operational systems to put in place.

b. Identifying routine tasks.

c. Ensuring ongoing operations are maintained.

d. Planning to achieve defined objectives.

46. Which one of the following statements <u>best</u> defines teamwork?

a. People working collaboratively towards a common goal.

b. Developing skills that will enhance project performance.

c. Gathering the right people together to work on a project.

d. Establishing vision and direction towards a common purpose.

47. A review undertaken to decide whether a project should proceed into its next phase is known as a:

a. Gate review.

b. Feasibility study.

c. Milestone review.

d. Evaluation review.

48. Which one of the following statements <u>best</u> describes the use of an issue log?

a. A summary of all possible alternative resolutions of an issue.

b. A summary of all the project issues, their analysis and status.

c. A tool to ensure that a process is in place for capturing all issues.

d. A tool to ensure that the issue management process is adhered to.

49. The <u>main</u> aim of a project risk management process should be to:

a. Identify project risks and then manage them appropriately.

b. Identify all project risks and transfer them immediately.

c. Identify all the things that are threats or opportunities on a project.

d. Satisfy the organisation's project management process.

50. What is a visual representation of a project's planned activities against a calendar called?

a. A Gantt chart.

b. A critical path precedence diagram.

c. A product flow diagram.

d. A Pareto chart.

FUNDAMENTALS

51. Configuration management is best described as:

a. Control in the implementation of changes to project schedules.

b. An organisation to review proposed changes to the project deliverables.

c. Quality control of project deliverables and documentation.

d. Creation, maintenance and controlled change of the project deliverables.

52. A cost breakdown structure (CBS) shows costs assigned to:

a. Individual work packages using the work breakdown structure (WBS).

b. Individual resources using the work breakdown structure (WBS).

c. Individual resources using the responsibility assignment matrix (RAM).

d. Individual deliverables using the responsibility assignment matrix (RAM).

53. The accuracy of an estimate should:

a. Decrease as a project progresses through its life cycle.

b. Increase as a project progresses through its life cycle.

c. Stay constant throughout the project life cycle.

d. Vary independently of where the project is in its life cycle.

54. Which one of the following best defines a benefit?

a. A positive result of stakeholder management.

b. The successful management of a project.

c. An improvement resulting from project deliverables.

d. The successful delivery of project reports and updates.

55. Which one of the following is true for the project management plan (PMP)?

a. The project management plan is developed by the project manager and team and owned by the sponsor.

b. A draft of the project management plan is developed by the sponsor at the same time as the business case.

c. The project management plan is developed by the sponsor and owned by the project manager.

d. The project management plan is developed by the project manager and team and owned by the project manager.

56. Who are project team members primarily accountable to?

a. External stakeholders.

b. The end users.

c. The finance director.

d. The project manager.

57. The phases of a project life cycle are:

a. Starting, planning, control and closing.

b. Concept, definition, development, handover and closure.

c. Initiation, definition, planning, monitoring and operations.

d. Concept, definition, implementation and operations.

58. A portfolio can <u>best</u> be defined as:

a. A group of projects and programmes carried out within an organisation.

b. A group of programmes carried out under the sponsorship of an organisation.

c. A group of projects carried out under the sponsorship of an organisation.

d. A range of products and services offered by an organisation.

59. Which one of the following <u>best</u> describes project management?

a. Using *APM's Body of Knowledge 6th edition* as a guide to all projects.

b. Employing a project manager who has undertaken similar projects.

c. Utilising team members who can work on a project full time.

d. Application of processes and methods throughout the project life cycle.

60. Which structure shows the reporting relationships and communications channels for a project?

a. Work breakdown structure.

b. Organisational breakdown structure.

c. Product breakdown structure.

d. Responsibility assignment structure.

Multiple-choice answers

1	2	3	4	5	6	7	8	9	10
B	C	D	A	A	A	A	D	C	A
11	12	13	14	15	16	17	18	19	20
C	B	B	B	C	D	B	C	B	B
21	22	23	24	25	26	27	28	29	30
A	C	A	A	C	B	A	C	C	A
31	32	33	34	35	36	37	38	39	40
B	A	B	D	A	D	D	B	C	B
41	42	43	44	45	46	47	48	49	50
C	C	D	A	D	A	A	B	A	A
51	52	53	54	55	56	57	58	59	60
D	A	B	C	D	D	B	A	D	B

Glossary of terms

This glossary contains terms derived from the *APM Body of Knowledge 6th edition*.

A

Accept
A response to a threat when no action is taken.

Acceptance criteria
The requirements and essential conditions that have to be achieved before a deliverable is accepted.

Activity
1. A task, job, operation or process consuming time and possibly other resources.
2. The smallest self-contained unit of work used to define the logic of a project.

Analogous estimating
See comparative estimating.

Analytical estimating
See bottom-up estimating.

Assurance
See quality assurance.

Avoid
A response to a threat that eliminates its probability or impact on the project.

B

Baseline
The reference levels against which a project, programme or portfolio is monitored and controlled.

Benefit
The quantifiable and measurable improvement resulting from completion of deliverables that is perceived as positive by a stakeholder. It will normally have a tangible value and be expressed in monetary terms that will justify the investment.

Benefits management
The identification, definition, planning, tracking and realisation of business benefits.

Board
A body that provides sponsorship to a project, portfolio or programme. The board will represent financial, provider and user interests.

Bottom-up estimating
An estimating technique that uses detailed specifications to estimate time and cost for each product or activity.

FUNDAMENTALS

Breakdown structure

A hierarchical structure by which project elements are broken down or decomposed. Examples include: cost breakdown structure (CBS), organisational breakdown structure (OBS), product breakdown structure (PBS) or work breakdown structure (WBS).

Business-as-usual

An organisation's normal day-to-day operations.

Business case

Provides justification for undertaking a project in terms of evaluating the benefits, cost and risk of alternative options and the rationale for the preferred solution.

C

Change control

The process through which all requests to change the baseline scope of a project, programme or portfolio are captured, evaluated and then approved, rejected or deferred.

Change register

A record of all project changes, proposed, authorised, rejected or deferred.

Change request

A request to obtain formal approval for changes to the scope of work.

Communication

The means by which information or instructions are exchanged. Successful communication occurs when the received meaning is the same as the transmitted meaning.

Comparative estimating

An estimating technique based on the comparison with, and factoring from, the cost of similar, previous work.

Concept (phase)

Concept is the first phase in the project or programme life cycle. During this phase the need, opportunity or problem is confirmed, the overall feasibility of the work considered and a preferred solution identified.

Configuration

Functional and physical characteristics of a deliverable defined in its specification.

Configuration management

Configuration management encompasses the administrative activities concerned with the creation, maintenance, controlled change and quality control of the scope of work.

Conflict management

The process of identifying and addressing differences that, if left unresolved, could affect objectives.

Consumable resource

A type of resource that only remains available until consumed (for example a material).

Context

A collective term for the governance and setting of a project, programme or portfolio.

Contingency

Resource set aside for responding to identified risks.

Contract

An agreement made between two or more parties that creates legally binding obligations between them. The contract sets out those obligations and the action that can be taken if they are not met.

Cost breakdown structure (CBS)

The hierarchical breakdown of a project into cost elements.

Critical path

A sequence of activities through a project precedence diagram from start to finish, the sum of whose durations determines the overall project duration. There may be more than one such path.

Critical path analysis

The procedure for calculating the critical path and floats in a precedence diagram.

D

Definition (phase)

The second phase of a project or programme life cycle where requirements are refined, the preferred solution is identified and ways of achieving it are identified.

Deliverable

A product, set of products or package of work that will be delivered to, and formally accepted by, a stakeholder.

E

Enhance

A response to an opportunity that increases its probability, impact or both.

Environment

The circumstances and conditions within which the project, programme or portfolio must operate.

Escalation

The process by which issues are drawn to the attention of a higher level of management.

Estimate

An approximation of time and cost targets, refined throughout the life cycle.

Estimating

The use of a range of tools and techniques to produce estimates.

Estimating funnel

A representation of the increasing levels of estimating accuracy that can be achieved through the phases of the life cycle.

Exploit

A response to an opportunity that maximises both its probability and its impact.

F

Finish-to-start

A dependency in an activity-on-node precedence diagram. It indicates that one activity cannot start until another activity has finished.

Float

A term used to describe the flexibility with which an activity may be rescheduled. There are various types of float, such as total float and free float.

G

Gantt chart

A graphical representation of activity against time. Variations may include information such as 'actual vs. planned', resource usage and dependencies.

Gate

The point between phases, gates and/or tranches where a go/no-go decision can be made about the remainder of the work.

Governance

The set of policies, regulations, functions, processes, procedures and responsibilities that define the establishment, management and control of projects, programmes and portfolios.

H

Handover

The point in the life cycle where deliverables are handed over to the sponsor and users.

Host organisation

The organisation that provides the strategic direction of the project, programme or portfolio and will be the primary recipient of the benefits.

I

Issue

A formal issue occurs when the tolerances of delegated work are predicted to be exceeded or have been exceeded. This triggers the escalation of the issue from one level of management to the next in order to seek a solution.

K

Key performance indicator (KPI)

Measure of success that can be used throughout the project to ensure that it is progressing towards a successful conclusion.

L

Leadership

The ability to establish vision and direction, to influence and align others towards a common purpose, and to empower and inspire people to achieve project success.

Lessons learned
Documented experiences that can be used to improve the future management of projects, programmes and portfolios.

M

Management plan
A plan that sets out the policies and principles that will be applied to the management of some aspects of a project, programme or portfolio. Examples include a risk management plan, a communication management plan and a quality management plan.

Milestone
A key event. An event selected for its importance to the project.

N

Negotiation
A discussion between two or more parties aimed at reaching agreement.

O

Objectives
Predetermined results towards which effort is directed. Objectives may be defined in terms of outputs, outcomes and/or benefits.

Operations management
The management of those activities that create the core services or products provided by an organisation.

Opportunity
A positive risk; a risk that if it occurs will have a beneficial effect on the project.

Organisation
The management structure applicable to the project, programme or portfolio and the organisational environment in which it operates.

Outcome
The changed circumstances or behaviour that results from the use of an output.

Output
The tangible or intangible product typically delivered by a project.

P

Parametric estimating
An estimating technique that uses a statistical relationship between historic data and other variables to calculate an estimate.

Phase
The major subdivision of a life cycle.

Planning
Determines what is to be delivered, how much it will cost, when it will be delivered, how it will be delivered and who will carry it out.

Portfolio
A grouping of an organisation's projects, programmes and related business-as-usual activities, taking into account resource constraints. Portfolios can be managed at an organisational or functional level.

Portfolio management
Portfolio management is the selection, prioritisation and control of an organisation's projects and programmes in line with its strategic objectives and capacity to deliver. The goal is to balance change initiatives and business-as-usual while optimising return on investment.

Precedence diagram
A network diagram in which activities are represented by rectangles (nodes) and their dependencies are represented by arrows.

Procurement
The process by which products and services are acquired from an external provider for incorporation into the project, programme or portfolio.

Product
A tangible or intangible component of a project's output. Synonymous with deliverable.

Programme
A group of related projects, which may include related business-as-usual activities that together achieve a beneficial change of a strategic nature for an organisation.

Programme management
Programme management is the coordinated management of projects and change management activities to achieve beneficial change.

Project
A unique, transient endeavour undertaken to achieve planned objectives.

Project environment
The circumstances and conditions within which the project, programme or portfolio must operate.

Project life cycle
A life cycle defines the inter-related phases of a project, programme or portfolio and provides a structure for governing the progression of the work.

Project management
The application of processes, methods, knowledge, skills and experience to achieve the project objectives.

Project management plan
The output of the definition phase of a project or programme.

Project sponsor
An important senior management role. The sponsor is accountable for ensuring that the work is governed effectively and delivers the objectives that meet identified needs.

Q

Quality
The fitness for purpose or the degree of conformance of the outputs of a process or the process itself.

Quality assurance
Provides confidence to the host organisation that its projects, programmes and portfolios are being well managed. It validates the consistent use of procedures and standards, and ensures that staff have the correct knowledge, skills and attitudes to fulfil their project roles and responsibilities in a competent manner.

Quality audit
An official examination to determine whether practices conform to specified standards or a critical analysis of whether a deliverable meets quality criteria.

Quality control
The process of monitoring specific project results to determine if they comply with relevant standards, and identifying ways to eliminate causes of unsatisfactory performance.

Quality management
A discipline for ensuring that outputs, benefits, and the processes by which they are delivered, meet stakeholder requirements and are fit for purpose.

Quality planning
The process of determining which quality standards are necessary and how to apply them.

R

Reduce
A response to a threat that reduces its probability, impact or both.

Reject
A response to an opportunity where no action is taken.

Resource management
The acquisition and deployment of the internal and external resources required to deliver the project, programme or portfolio.

Resources
All those items required to undertake work including people, finance and materials.

Resource scheduling
A collection of techniques used to calculate the resources required to deliver the work and when they will be required.

FUNDAMENTALS

Responsibility assignment matrix (RAM)

A diagram or chart showing assigned responsibilities for elements of work. It is created by combining the work breakdown structure with the organisational breakdown structure.

Re-usable resource

A resource that, when no longer needed, becomes available for other uses. Accommodation, machines, test equipment and people are re-usable.

Reviews

A review is a critical evaluation of a deliverable, business case or P3 management process.

Risk

The potential of an action or event to impact on the achievement of objectives.

Risk event

An uncertain event or set of circumstances that would, if it occurred, have an effect on the achievement of one or more objectives.

Risk management

A process that allows individual risk events and overall risk to be understood and managed proactively, optimising success by minimising threats and maximising opportunities.

Risk register

A document listing identified risk events and their corresponding planned responses.

S

Schedule

A timetable showing the forecast start and finish dates for activities or events within a project, programme or portfolio.

Scope

The totality of the outputs, outcomes and benefits and the work required to produce them.

Scope management

The process whereby outputs, outcomes and benefits are identified defined and controlled.

Share

A response to an opportunity that increases its probability, impact or both by sharing the risk with a third party.

Stage

A sub-division of the development phase of a project created to facilitate approval gates at suitable points in the life cycle.

Stakeholder

The organisations or people who have an interest or role in the project, programme or portfolio or are impacted by it.

Stakeholder management

The systematic identification, analysis, planning and implementation of actions designed to engage with stakeholders.

Success criteria

The qualitative or quantitative measures by which the success of project management is judged.

Success factors

Management practices that, when implemented, will increase the likelihood of success of a project, programme or portfolio.

T

Teamwork

A group of people working in collaboration or by cooperation towards a common goal.

Threat

A negative risk event; a risk event that if it occurs will have a detrimental effect on the objectives.

Time scheduling

A collection of techniques used to develop and present schedules that show when work will be performed.

Tolerance

A permissible variation in performance parameters.

Total float

Time by which an activity may be delayed or extended without affecting the total project duration or violating a target finish date.

Transfer

A response to a threat that reduces its probability, impact or both by transferring the risk to a third party.

U

Users

The group of people who are intended to receive benefits or operate outputs.

W

Work package

A group of related activities that are defined at the same level within a work breakdown structure.

Index

FUNDAMENTALS

FUNDAMENTALS